HOME BUYING 101:

What They Don't Teach You in the Classroom

D1527697

HOME BUYING 101:

What They Don't Teach You in the Classroom

Abduljabar I. Totonji

ISBN: 979-8-6646-9731-5

For questions, comments, or inquires, contact the author at
Abduljabar@GoldenEagleGroup.net

Printed in the United States of America

Disclaimer

The information provided in this publication does not, and is not intended to, constitute legal advice, and should not be relied upon in lieu of consultation with appropriate legal advisers in the appropriate jurisdiction. This book should not be a substitute for direct, personalized, and relevant advice from an attorney, financial adviser, real estate agent, or escrow/closing agent. Although the author and publisher have made every effort to ensure that the information in this book is correct and accurate, the author and publisher do not assume, and hereby disclaim, any liability to any party for any loss, damage, or disruption caused by errors or omissions, whether such errors or omissions result from negligence, accident, or any other cause. The publisher and author bear no responsibility for any real estate or financial transaction undertaken by the reader. Purchasing this book does not create a fiduciary or professional relationship with the publisher or author. The publication may not be entirely capture current laws and practices as the subject matter changes frequently and is subject to wide variability among jurisdictions. Please consult with a licensed attorney or real estate professionals regarding any financial or real estate transactions you plan on making.

To my wife and partner, Sara, who helped me build a real estate empire and inspires me to do better every single day.

To my parents, Irfan and Ghazwa, who taught me the importance of hard work, education, and how to buy my first home.

Table of Contents

Chapter 4: Making an Offer

Chapter 5: Post Ratified Contract

Chapter 6: Closing

Chapter 7: Post Purchase

Chapter 8: Home Buying Recommendations

Appendix A: Home Buying Time Frame

Introduction

*The ache for home lives in all of us, the safe place
where we can go as we are and not be questioned.*
—Maya Angelou

During my early childhood, my parents ingrained in
my siblings and me two essential ideas that would
go on to pave the way to our financial independence.
First and foremost, "Invest in your education and
self-improvement with your time or money." Second-
ly, "The most important purchase you should make
toward bettering your future is a home."

My parents immigrated to the United States with
no money, barely any English, and a baby boy (not
me, but my older brother). While they were educated
and financially stable in their home country, they came
to the United States in search of freedom and a more
opportunistic future for their children. They worked
their butts off, to put it mildly. Like many hardwork-
ing immigrants, they spent their days at one job and
nights at another. My brother and I spent our days at
school and nights in the family van, studying, building

forts, and sleeping while they worked. Those "hard, harsh days" as my father would later refer to them, paid off. My parents went on to build a very successful national real estate investment firm.

You could say I grew up in an energetic environment, where I watched everyone around me grind. We were encouraged to do our best in school and to take on whatever sports and extracurricular activities we could handle. My mom would quote a famous saying by Prophet Muhammed (PBUH), "God loves that when anyone of you does a job, he should perfect it." I took these words to heart, and they molded me into who I am today.

My parents also encouraged an entrepreneurial spirit within the household. When I was eight years old, I started breeding cockatiel birds and selling them at a local pet shop. I was making around $300 a month. For a little boy with no overhead, I felt like a millionaire. From that moment on, I saved every penny. In middle school and high school, I spent my summers on construction sites, laying brick, framing homes, putting up drywall, cleaning, and painting. My youth was filled with early mornings, hot days, and lots of manual labor. It was hard work, but those long hours helped me build a modest savings account, which would eventually become the down payment for my first home. It also helped me appreciate the tremendous effort construction workers put in, day in and day out.

When you're rooted in an entrepreneurial environment, you learn things at a young age that most kids wouldn't normally even consider. I had a checking account when I turned fifteen, and I applied for a credit card on my eighteenth birthday so I could start building credit responsibly. My parents taught my siblings and me to pay the balance of a credit card off at the end of each month. As a result of this environment, I learned the perils of borrowing, the benefits of investing, the fundamentals of taxes, and how to buy real estate.

I've always wondered why these essential life lessons weren't taught in school. The concepts seem so fundamentally crucial to a financially independent life, yet they are often excluded from the curriculum. In high school, I would ask of each subject, "How is this going to help me in the future?" Why did we have to learn about the Pythagorean theorem and osmosis while learning financial independence wasn't even an option or elective? I wanted to know how to become financially independent, make investments, and properly pay taxes. I was curious about how to read a contract, the benefits of buying versus leasing a car or home, and how to buy my first home one day. You know, the stuff that applies to *everyone* but isn't taught in the classroom.

I decided early on that I would one day write a book that captures the critical decisions related to buying a home. This is that book. My intention in what follows is to help those with the same questions I had before purchasing my first home. You'll realize three things about this book right away, all of which are intentional. The first is that it's short. My intent is to have you, the reader, be able to pick it up and read it in a few hours, without any fluff or irrelevant information—after all, time is money! The second is that the tone of the book is informal and conversational. Buying a home is complicated enough, no need to make the language complicated, too. The goal is to present the steps to homeownership with my own advice in the most straightforward way possible. The third is that I love quotations! Throughout the book, you'll see some of my favorite quotations regarding home buying, quotations that will give you a different perspective on the process. I've also included a Glossary and Acronyms list at the end of this book in case there's a word you're not familiar with.

If you don't finish the book or you get bored halfway through (it happens), I would suggest that you at least read the last chapter, "Home Buying Recommendations." This chapter offers a distillation of my personal "Home Buying Tips" that could save you time and money down the road.

One last thought I want to share with you before we get into the nuts and bolts of home buying: out of all the books available to you, I am honored and humbled that you have chosen to read this one. Thank you! I sincerely hope you extract information that will demonstrate to you the value of homeownership, while avoiding some of the most common pitfalls home buyers face. With that intro out of the way, let's get started!

Chapter 1:

Buying versus Renting

I will forever believe that buying a home is a great investment. Why? Because you can't live in a stock certificate. You can't live in a mutual fund.
— Oprah Winfrey

Not a week goes by without me hearing the question, "Is buying a home really better than renting?" The simple answer is yes. However, like anything else in life, it depends on your specific situation. Some of the factors you should consider are how long you plan on living at the home, your debt-to-income ratio, market conditions, and so on. Overall, buying a home sets you on the path to financial freedom. So, yes, if you're able to make it happen, buying is a better choice than renting. Here's why:

1. Property Appreciation

There is only so much land available. Earth's geological process creates new land and erodes old land at an agonizingly slow pace. This finitude of land resources is one reason real estate investors always emphasize "location, location, location." There are only so many homes you can fit into New York City, for example. Because it's one of the busiest and most historic cities in the world and a city that attracts thousands of new residents every year, New York City is one of the most expensive places to live on the globe. The simple economic law of supply and demand keeps property prices and rent rising, so long as the demand remains high. As of January 2020, the most expensive home ever sold in America was a jaw-dropping 24,000 square foot New York City penthouse that sold for $238,000,000[1]. That's almost $10,000 per square foot. Crazy!

The extremely limited space within New York City drives the property market up faster and faster every year. Like a runaway train, the property market keeps steaming forward. Since the 1940s, the United States' population has doubled, and the median home price has quadrupled in value. No surprise there. The short-term growth rates may change; however, the long-term trajectory is clear. The graphs below (figs. 1, 2) from the United States Census Bureau chart the cur-

1 Katherine Clarke. "Billionaire Ken Griffin Buys America's Most Expensive Home for $238 Million." *The Wall Street Journal,* Dow Jones & Company, January 23, 2019. www.wsj.com/articles/billionaire-ken-griffin-buys-americas-most-expensive-home-for-238-million-11548271301.

rent population and median home price increase, as well as the expected trend over the next thirty years.

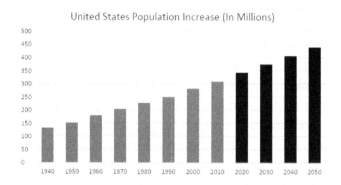

Figure 1: *United States Population Increase (In Millions), US Census Bureau*

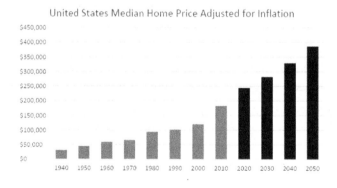

Figure 2: *United States Median Home Price Adjusted for Inflation. US Census Bureau).*

2. Building Monthly Equity

In his *New York Times* best-selling book, *The Automatic Millionaire*, David Bach writes, "As a renter, you can easily spend half a million dollars or more on rent over the years ($1,500 a month for thirty years comes to $540,000), and in the end wind up just where you started—owning nothing. Or you can buy a house and spend the same amount paying down a mortgage, and in the end, wind up owning your own home free and clear!"[2] If you can manage the down payment, you will save yourself and your family from a substantial financial burden long term by buying rather than renting. After mustering up 20 percent of the overall purchasing price required as a down payment, you just make payments as if you're paying rent—the major difference is that by buying you'll become a property owner in the end, with lucrative tax-deductible benefits. Think about it; everyone needs a place to live. If you don't own, you have to rent. It's as simple as that. Why not let your monthly payments work for you?

On a thirty-year fixed mortgage, your payment will be a flat rate every month. That payment is split between interest, principal, and escrow. Each month, the interest portion of your mortgage decreases while the principal portion increases. A $375,000 home with 20 percent down and a 5 percent interest rate would have an interest and principal payment of $1,610 per month. As time progresses, that would be split as follows:

2   David Bach, *The Automatic Millionaire: a Powerful One-Step Plan to Live and Finish Rich* (New York: Currency Press, 2016)

Month 1	Month 60	Month 120
Interest: $1,250	Interest: $1,150	Interest: $1,020
Principal: $360	Principal: $460	Principal: $590

When paying a mortgage, you're essentially paying off your loan a little faster each month. Consequently, your net worth increases every month!

3. Tax Deductions

Real estate is the most effective way to make money while paying the least amount of taxes. In fact, the American tax system is more favorable to individuals whose primary source of income is derived from capital gains, probably as a way to incentivize people to invest in properties, while promoting "the American Dream." Regardless of the reason, you should take advantage of it.

Paying rent yields no real financial advantages and no tax deductions. Paying your mortgage, in contrast, offers many financial benefits. For instance, any interest you pay on your mortgage is deductible from your taxes. Using the same example from above, a $375,000 home with a 20 percent down payment and a 5 percent interest rate, would equal $14,900 for one year of interest payments. All of that is tax-deductible. If your state has real estate property taxes, these are most likely tax-deductible as well. Let's say you want to complete a few renovations. Are you planning to paint the house, add a fence, or do any other remodeling that would raise the value of your home?

Make sure you keep those receipts, because the cost of renovations can be deducted from your property gains tax when you sell the property.

4. Wealth and Security

After studying the habits of millionaires for years, Dr. Thomas J. Stanley, author of *The Millionaire Next Door,* determined the following regarding the "average" millionaire: "Most of us (97 percent) are homeowners. We live in homes currently valued at an average of $320,000. About half of us have occupied the same home for more than twenty years. Thus, we have enjoyed significant increases in the value of our homes."[3] It's no coincidence that 97 percent of millionaires are homeowners. Real estate is one of the most expensive and appreciating assets on the market, and most millionaires use it to not only maintain but to increase their net worth. Generally, the word "investment" is associated with real estate or the stock market. Both avenues serve as tried and true methods for creating and preserving wealth. I'm not an expert on stocks so we'll stick to real estate and homeownership for now.

In this book, we'll analyze a specific scenario to better understand the benefits of buying a home. This will help clarify why the majority of millionaires own instead of rent. Additionally, we'll examine how purchasing a home saves you money and speeds up

3   Thomas J. Stanley and William D. Danko, *The Millionaire Next Door: The Surprising Secrets of America's Wealthy* (Lanham, MD: Taylor Trade Publishing, 1996)

your access to the coveted millionaire's club, or even just financial independence. To avoid the "that's not a realistic comparison" excuse, we'll reference a personal and real scenario later in this chapter.

5. Freedom and Control

Homeownership provides a sense of pride and commitment to your community, but being a homeowner also gives you a feeling of control and freedom. You'll never worry about anyone coming into your home in the middle of the day for an inspection. You'll never worry about defaulting on your lease, reporting to your landlord, negotiating your lease renewal, or seeing an unexpected price jump in the rent. You can paint the wall whatever color you choose. You're in complete control, with no one to answer to. All these benefits and conveniences are priceless, especially for your sanity.

Now, let's take a look at a pair of scenarios that will help illustrate the benefits of buying a home.

Renting Scenario

Mr. and Mrs. Tenant are looking for a property for themselves and their two kids. The family of four has saved $75,000, but they're not convinced that buying a home is the right move. They're considering investing the $75,000 in stocks and bonds that generate an average 6 percent annual return. While on the hunt for a new home, they find the perfect property, a three-bedroom townhome. They fall in love with it and apply to lease the property. The landlord accepts their application, and they sign a one-year lease agreement. Mr. and Mrs. Tenant pay $100 for their application and $1,000 in moving costs, and they agree to $2,350 in rental payments across a twelve-month term.

As you might expect, the family really enjoys living in their townhome. The schools are great, their kids make friends with the neighbors, and things are going well. The family thinks, "Let's lease it for one more year, why not?" All that is left is to contact Mr. Landlord, who is always happy to hear when tenants want to renew their lease. In fact, this time, the market has been good to Mr. Landlord—home values in the neighborhood have increased!

He agrees to renew but tells the Tenants that similar properties are now leasing for $2,500 per month. That's an additional $150 per month, or $1,800 a year! While that extra $150 per month may not break the bank, it is meaningful when you think of it from an opportunity cost perspective: with $1,800 a year you can get smart home gadgets, or change the tile in your bathroom, and a whole lot more.

What choice does the family have? Pack up and find another place? In the middle of the school year? Pay another $100 application fee and $1,000 in moving costs? What about minor inconveniences like updating driver's licenses, updating bank checks, and even calling the cable company? Who wants to deal with the cable company? It's a tough decision. $1,800 is a lot of money; however, the Tenants decide, "You know what? It's worth it!" They sign that new lease agreement and boom, they're in it for another year.

Another great year passes by. The children grow; the family's footprint in the community becomes more significant. Now, the Tenants are completely attached to "their" beloved home. Meanwhile, Mr. Landlord's property appreciates again in the strong economy, and one particular property in the neighborhood sells for a record price. That's all the justification Mr. Landlord needs to think his home should be rented for $2,700. Another $200 increase? This is too much for Mr. and Mrs. Tenant. When the second year comes to an end, they both agree it's not worth it; it's just too much! A similar house three miles away is on the market for $2,400 a month. The new home would save them $100 a month from their current rent of $2,500 and staying where they are would now be $300 a month more expensive. The family decides that the cost and nuisance of moving are now justified.

After applying for the new home, they get accepted and move. On their move-out day, Mr. Landlord performs a standard move-out inspection. He spots some missing door stoppers, some crayon-colored walls, and a large coffee stain in the master bedroom. All in all, it costs $850 to get these things taken care of. After deducting the damages from the Tenant's security deposit, the family gets back $1,500 of their original $2,350 deposit.

The Tenants have learned from their mistakes and are smarter this time around. They sign a three-year fixed lease, guaranteeing no escalations above $2,400 monthly for three years. Their new home is a little older than their last, which is why they got such a good price, but the biggest drawback is that their son's school district changes during the middle of the school year. Even so, the family takes pride in the fact that the backyard is larger. This space provides an emotional haven against the uprooted feeling that results from moving houses. To further ease the separation anxiety, the family decides to get a puppy, Biscuit, to help their son acclimate to the new school change. Biscuit's energy reverberates throughout the house and invigorates their spirits. The transition doesn't feel so bad anymore. If Biscuit would stop getting lost around the neighborhood, things might just be perfect.

What the family needs is a fence. They call the owner and plead their case. The only problem is that Mr. Landlord doesn't see the value of installing a $3,000 fence. The head of the household, Mr. Tenant, takes a moment to ask himself, "Do I really want to spend $3,000 on a fence while on a three-year lease? That would be enhancing the value of the property for the landlord. This isn't really my home, we just rent." At that moment, it hits him: two years ago, they could have taken their $75,000 and invested in a property to call their own. Instead, the family is forced to adapt to life in an open backyard, along with many other modifications unsuitable to their preferences.

This narrative paints a vivid picture of what life is like when you decide to rent over purchasing a home.

You're never really in control when you're leasing. You'll always be at the mercy of the landlord's will. As long as the landlord is staying within the terms of the lease, he or she may inspect the property, market it for sale, renovate it, or take other actions that may be a distraction or inconvenience to you or your family.

Keeping the aforementioned scenario in mind, let's take a closer look at the Tenants' financial situation after five years with a simple chart (fig. 3):

Renting	Year 1	Year 2	Year 3	Year 4	Year 5	Five Year Total
Application Fee	$ 100	$ -	$ 100	$ -	$ -	$ 200
Moving Costs	$ 1,000	$ -	$ 1,000	$ -	$ -	$ 2,000
Rent	$ 28,200	$ 30,000	$ 28,800	$ 28,800	$ 29,400	$ 145,200
Security Deposit	$ 2,350	$ (1,500)	$ 2,400	$ -	$ (2,400)	$ 850
Total	$ 31,650	$ 28,500	$ 32,300	$ 28,800	$ 27,000	$ 148,250

Figure 3: *The Tenants' Finances after Five Years*

Let's not forget, they did invest their $75,000, which generated a 6 percent return, compounded every year (fig. 4):

	Year 1	Year 2	Year 3	Year 4	Year 5	Total
Investment	$ 4,500	$ 4,770	$ 5,056	$ 5,360	$ 5,681	$ 25,367
Net Cost	$ 27,150	$ 23,730	$ 27,244	$ 23,440	$ 21,319	$ 122,883

Figure 4: *The Tenants' Investment over Five Years*

If their investment yielded a 6 percent return per year, and they received their full deposit back after year five, the Tenants would have spent a total of $122,883 in five years. That averages out to a net cost of just under $25,000 a year. Not a bad financial situation, but could it have been better? Let's take a look at another scenario.

Home Buying Analysis

Assuming a homeowner purchased a $375,000 home with 20 percent down ($75,000) and a 5 percent interest fee on a thirty-year fixed loan (if some of this doesn't make sense now, don't worry—we'll come back to it), they would be looking at the following payments (fig. 5):

Purchasing	Year 1	Year 2	Year 3	Year 4	Year 5	Five Year Total
Moving Costs	$ 1,000	$ -	$ -	$ -	$ -	$ 1,000
HOA Fees	$ 1,000	$ 1,030	$ 1,061	$ 1,093	$ 1,126	$ 5,309
Real Estate Taxes	$ 3,750	$ 3,825	$ 3,902	$ 3,980	$ 4,059	$ 19,515
Mortgage Payment	$ 19,325	$ 19,325	$ 19,325	$ 19,325	$ 19,325	$ 96,625
Total Expense	$ 25,075	$ 24,180	$ 24,287	$ 24,397	$ 24,510	$ 122,449

Figure 5: *Total Expense of Purchasing Home over Five Years*

The mortgage payment is comprised of both interest and principal. Principal pays off your loan effectively, serving as a "savings" account, if you will. Historically, with some exceptions, real estate has consistently appreciated over time. Therefore, we can conservatively assume 2 percent appreciation per year. The interest portion of your mortgage payment, along with the real estate tax payments are all also tax-deductible. Based on those figures, let's assume a 20 percent return. Taking all that into consideration gives us a net cost of $48,700, which is just under $10,000 a year.

Mortgage Principal Payback	$	4,426	$	4,652	$	4,890	$	5,140	$	5,404	$ 24,512
Home Value Increase	$	-	$	7,500	$	7,650	$	7,803	$	7,959	$ 30,912
Return on Interest and Real Estate Tax Deduction (20%)	$	3,730	$	3,700	$	3,667	$	3,633	$	3,596	$ 18,326
Total Investment Return	$	8,156	$	15,852	$	16,207	$	16,576	$	16,959	$ 73,750
Net Cost	$	16,919	$	8,328	$	8,080	$	7,821	$	7,551	$ 48,700

Figure 6: *Net Cost of Purchasing Home over Five Years*

Over five years, that's a $75,000 difference between leasing and buying, and the gap will keep growing larger and larger every year. But buying a home is a long-term investment. If you plan to live in a place for only a year or two, don't buy it! Wait until you're ready to make a long-term commitment. Price appreciation is a long-term goal, as it's hard to time the market just right to maximize your return in the short-term, and closing costs, inspections, broker commissions, etc., will eat into your profits.

The buying-versus-renting debate is specific to an individual's needs or situation, but from a financial and investment standpoint, you are better off in the long run purchasing a home than paying rent. 97 percent of millionaires own their homes, not because they are rich, but because buying a home helped them become rich.

Chapter 2:

Preparing Your Finances

*Do not save what is left after spending, but spend
what is left after saving.*

—Warren Buffet

How prepared are you? Getting your ducks in a row,
as they say, is one of the most significant barriers to
homeownership. You'll want to prepare your finances
to make the process as seamless as possible. Don't
worry; it's not rocket science. Follow these simple
steps to get where you need to be.

Step 1: Know Your Situation

First and foremost, please stay away from rule-of-
thumb scenarios, which don't take into account
your specific situation and personal needs. For example, "Your monthly mortgage payment should not

exceed 28 percent of your gross monthly income."
Who comes up with this stuff? Let's say, for instance,
that Couple A has a dual income of $100,000 with no
kids and only $500 per month in other debt payments
(student loans, cars, etc.), while Couple B, who also
make $100,000 a year, has three kids and $2,000 in
additional debt payments per month. Can they both
afford to spend 28 percent of their monthly income
on a mortgage? No idea. We don't know the full picture. Everyone's situation is unique. As tempting as
it is to follow a standard approach that people say is
"the right way," don't! Analyze your situation and seek
help from a certified financial adviser if you're having
doubts.

Here are some things to consider so that you can
identify your specific situation:

- **Get Ready to Bear the Costs of Homeownership.**
  Understanding the benefits of being a homeowner will make the costs seem 100 percent worth
  the investment. If you've already read Chapter 1,
  you're ahead of the game. I told you this was easy.
- **Calculate the Amount of the Largest Down
  Payment You Can Reasonably Make.**
  Let's be honest; there isn't a universally accepted rule to calculate how much you can afford to
  pay as a down payment. You'll just have to think
  critically. Take a detailed snapshot of your finances. What are your monthly obligations? How
  much discretionary income do you spend? You'll

want to have a good idea of your financial situation to properly assess what you can afford to put down. More importantly, be realistic. If you're reading this, you're probably an adult and fully understand what your responsibilities are. While buying a home can come with some incredible benefits, spreading yourself too thin can cause terrible stress. To avoid that, simply think realistically about how large of a down payment you can make. You'll be able to calculate your down payment by completing the following:

- **Calculate Your Debt-to-Income Ratio.**
  Your debt-to-income ratio is calculated by dividing your monthly debt obligations by your monthly gross income. The ratio is expressed as a percentage, and lenders use it to determine how well you manage monthly debts (and if you'll be able to repay your loan). The lower your debt-to-income ratio, the more attractive a candidate you become. According to Fannie Mae, lenders prefer to see a debt-to-income ratio of less than 36 percent, with no more than 28 percent of that debt going toward servicing your mortgage.[4]

  Once calculated, work on lowering your debt-to-income ratio by paying off any small debts you may have. If you are still unsure how to calculate it, there are endless calcu-

---

4   "Selling Guide," B3-6-02, Debt-to-Income Ratios, Fannie Mae, accessed February 5, 2020, https://selling-guide.fanniemae.com/.

lators on the web to help you out.

- **Break Down Your Fixed Expenses**.

  Most people can list off the items they pay each month by heart. If you can't recall every expense, perhaps it's time to consider scaling back. Think long and hard about all your bills, subscriptions, and responsibilities (e.g., phone bills, Netflix). By going through your statements, you'll be able to make a complete list of fixed costs. You may be surprised to find some potential savings opportunities as well.

- **Build an Iron-Clad Budget.**

  Sit down and analyze where your money is actually going. A quick analysis can reveal ways to cut back. You want to take a deep look at how much, how frequently, and on what you're spending money. Often, this process will uncover patterns or trends of which you may not have been aware. Break it all down into categories, as many credit cards already do on your monthly statements. You can also get dynamic with your budgeting by using an app to manage everything down to the last penny. Develop budgeting habits that ensure you reach your goals. Check out Mint.com or EveryDollar.com for a free app to implement a working budget.

- **Don't Forget About Your Safety Net.**

  Here's a tip you don't want to overlook: your down payment will require a sizable chunk of savings, but it should be just that, a chunk, not the whole pie. Save a safety net for a minimum of three months' worth of living expenses. You never know what life will throw at you—from job loss to unexpected health problems, anything can happen. Having a three-month safety net gives you time to figure it out.

Step 2: Know the Extra Costs Involved in Buying a House

There are always smaller supplemental costs to any sizable or substantial purchase. When you buy a new phone, you'll end up getting a case, perhaps the protection plan, and maybe some other accessories. Similarly, cruise lines and restaurants sometimes add mandatory service fees. The same is true when buying a home. The added fees can quickly mount up, and you need to be aware of them. Here are some of the fees associated with buying a home:

- **Appraisal Fee**
  When financing a loan, your lender will probably demand a home inspection by a certified appraiser. Ask your lender how much they'll charge to get an exact price. If you're buying your home with cash, you can ask your agent to recommend a certified appraiser.
- **Closing Costs**
  The term "closing costs" is a category that encompasses many distinct fees associated with

closing on a property purchase. Some of the fees that might be associated with your closing are pest inspection fees, recordation fees, county, or state taxes, Homeowner's Association (HOA) initiation fees, etc.

- **Escrow**

  Some lenders will require you to put a couple months' worth of property taxes, mortgage insurance, and property insurance in an escrow account at closing. An escrow account is managed by a third party where money is held or accumulated until a bill becomes due.

- **Home Inspection**

  You're about to spend hundreds of thousands, perhaps millions, on your home. You owe it to yourself to have an in-depth inspection performed. To ensure a quality inspection, make sure you opt for an inspector certified by the American Society of Home Inspectors. Ensuring a home is in great condition, for such a significant investment, will always be money well spent.

- **HOA or Condo Fees**

  Your dream property just might be in a master association or condominium building that maintains the property's amenities. These added services might include exterior landscaping, elevator maintenance, electricity, water bills, swimming pool, management office, playground, etc. Just make sure you know what the HOA or condo is covering and the associated monthly costs. There may also be a one-time setup fee charged at closing. You will need to look over the guidelines, rules, and stipulations in detail.

- **Immediate Repairs or Maintenance**

  Just because you've had a home inspection done, that doesn't mean the inspector will catch everything. Things like appliances can be in good condition one day and break a month later. Additionally, some things like windows, drywall, or light fixtures may break during the move-in process, so make sure to put aside a small amount of money to take care of any emergencies.

- **Lender Fees**

  This is one of the less enjoyable parts of the home buying experience. Lenders have fees. These are usually a range of small fees that add up to a hefty sum. Have your lender break it down and provide you with an estimate before you sign on the dotted lines. You can expect administrative fees, document fees, escrow fees, and filing fees.

- **Real Property Tax**

  This will be an ongoing yearly tax paid to your county. Usually the annual real property tax is lumped into your monthly mortgage payment, where the lender will put the money aside in an escrow account until they are due. Taxes will vary from state to state and county to county. Refer to your county's real estate division and lender for costs associated with your potential home. It's good to note that the majority of your real property tax payments go to public schools, maintenance of public roads, parks, and libraries.

- **Title Insurance**

  This is the cost for the title insurance policy, which is a one-time payment and covers you for as long as you own the home.

- **Transfer Tax**

  This is the tax associated with transferring the title from the seller to the buyer. In theory, it's comparable to sales tax on anything you might purchase from a store. Taxes will vary from state to state. You can always ask the closing agent and lender for state-specific taxes. For most questions regarding the details and costs involved with your loan, refer to your county's real estate division, closing agent, and lender.

- **Other Miscellaneous Expenses:**

  There are a bunch of other fees or costs associated with purchasing a home like supplemental tax or utility bills, a master planned community fee, or parking fees to name a few. Each property is different so make sure to ask the seller and your agent to check for any costs associated with your specific property.

Step 3: Know How Credit Scores Can Affect Mortgage Interest Rates

If you're not already closely tracking your credit score, you should start now. The higher your credit score, the lower your interest rate will be. When considering a thirty-year loan for potentially hundreds of thousands of dollars, a quarter- or half-percent increase in your interest rate can cost tens of thousands of dollars in additional interest charges. Credit scores will range between 300 and 850. Lenders use this score to determine how likely someone is to repay their loan. As you may already know, your credit score is calculated using your credit history. The better your history, the higher your score. Here's a table from Experian (fig. 7) showing credit score brackets and the percentage of Americans in each.

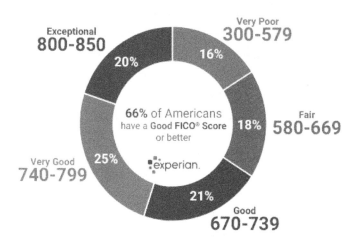

Figure 7: *"Percentage of Americans in Each Credit Score Bracket," Experian.*

Want to find out where you stand? Websites like CreditKarma.com offer great tools for learning your score, payment history, and suggestions on how to improve your score. If you've always been debt free or have no sources of building credit, you'll discover that you may not have a score. While being debt free is great, not having a credit score isn't, and your mortgage options will be limited as a result.

If you're like the 34 percent of Americans with a score under 670, you'll want to work on improving that score. Alternatively, you can find a lender who practices manual underwriting, which will help you get a mortgage without relying on a credit score. Churchill Mortgage is an example of a mortgage company that endorses this practice. For the rest of us, here are some basic factors that may affect your score:

- **Payment History**

  Late or missed payments are the most damaging factor to credit scores. A few late payments can really ruin all that hard work you've been doing. Apps like Mint.com or Bill Tracker can help you keep track of any outstanding bills. Making sure you pay on time is the first step to improving your score. Any debt collections like utility bills, old gym memberships, or library fees could hurt you. If you have any outstanding expenses, pay them as soon as you can.

- **Total Debt and Accounts**

  Debt is a finely crafted concept that, when leveraged correctly, can enhance your quality of life. On one hand, if you have too much debt, lenders will be hesitant to loan you more money, as this debt could overburden you. On the other hand, too little debt history and there won't be enough evidence to show how responsible you are at completing your financial obligations. My opinion? Try to have as little debt as possible. Paying off your debt shows that you'll actually pay back what you owe. The more accounts you open and pay off, the better your score will get. Having a credit card that you pay in full every month, for instance, is a good way to build credit.

- **Age of Credit History**
  The longer you can show on-time payments, the better. Having a long-standing history (over ten years) is better than a year or two. This shows lenders that, overall, you lead a stable life, without much financial fluctuation. That will be important to consider when a lender is evaluating your thirty-year mortgage application.

- **Hard Inquiries**
  When your credit is pulled by a lender, seller, or landlord for review, you're usually looking to obtain more debt. This can be anything from a car to an apartment, or even credit cards. The lenders and underwriters will need to take a deep look at your credit history. These hard inquiries will usually hurt your score for a very short amount of time (three to six months).

- **Credit Card Utilization**
  Credit cards typically come with a limit on how

much you can spend each month. If you're spending anything over 35 percent of that limit per month, you're hurting your score. For example, let's say your American Express card has a $10,000 monthly limit. If you're spending more than $3,500 on that card, you'll be negatively affecting your score. The rationale behind this is that even though you can spend up to $10,000 doesn't mean you should. Not utilizing your full credit limit shows lenders how responsible you really are. A cool trick that could help is to call your credit card company about every six months and ask them to increase your credit limit. Getting your utilization down to 10 percent is how you'll start boosting your score. Another cool trick is to pay off as much as you can of your credit card balance before your statement is reported to the credit agencies. This way your low balance is what gets reported and counted towards your credit utilization.

- **Ignoring Potential Inaccuracies**

The last thing you want to do is bear the brunt of credit inaccuracies. They do happen, and you need to avoid them as much as possible. If you're regularly checking your credit score, you might notice some discrepancies or errors in your credit history. Someone with a similar name or social security number may have been coded to your account. The credit bureaus Experian, Equifax, and Transunion are required to investigate any disputes that are submitted due to the Fair Credit Reporting Act. If you notice any errors, report them because they could have a significant negative impact on your score.

Step 4: Know the Various Types of Mortgages

If you've completed the first three steps, you should have a clearer idea of how much your monthly payments are going to be, but you still need to understand the various types of mortgages and select which one you want. Your loan officer will present several different options on how to structure your loan. Generally, there are four types of mortgages to choose from: conventional, government-insured, adjustable-rate mortgages (ARM), and sharia-compliant mortgages.

Conventional Mortgages

There are two different forms of conventional (or fixed) mortgages. These are known as conforming and nonconforming. A conforming loan classifies your loan amount under the limits set forth by Fannie Mae or Freddie Mac. For those who don't know, Fannie Mae and Freddie Mac were created by Congress to provide liquidity, stability, and affordability to the mortgage market[5]. If your loan exceeds those limits, it is classified as nonconforming. Conventional loans are

5   "About Fannie Mae & Freddie Mac," Federal Housing Finance Agency, accessed May 20, 2020, https://www.fhfa.gov/SupervisionRegulation/FannieMaeand-FreddieMac/Pages/About-Fannie-Mae---Freddie-Mac.aspx.

the most common since they can be used for primary, vacation, and investment properties. Buyers making down payments of less than 20 percent will be required to pay primary mortgage insurance (PMI). PMI usually costs anywhere between 0.5 percent to 1.0 percent of the loan amount annually. As an example, if you buy a $500,000 home and put $50,000 down (10 percent), your loan balance would be $450,000. PMI costs will range between $2,250 to $4,500 per year or $187.50 to $375.00 per month.

Advantages of Conventional Mortgages
- The total cost involved with borrowing is typically lower. This holds true even when interest rates might be above average.
- If your down payment was less than 20 percent, you could request your lender to eliminate PMI once you have accrued 20 percent equity.
- Certain government-backed loans allow you to pay as little as 3 percent down.

Disadvantages of Conventional Mortgages
- Prepare yourself for a lengthy documentation process that will verify income, assets, down payment, and employment.
- Your credit score needs to be higher than 620.
- Your credit history must show a debt-to-income ratio between 45 to 50 percent.
- In the case that your down payment is lower than 20 percent, you will most likely be required to pay PMI.

Who Should Get a Conventional Mortgage?

Anyone buying a home that doesn't qualify for a government-sponsored loan should consider a conventional mortgage. Whether you've missed payments, have too much debt, or don't have enough credit history, you may be one of the many Americans with a credit score of less than 620. As discussed in Step 3, you should first focus on improving your credit score by paying off small debts or acquiring an authorized tradeline. The "Debt-Snowball Strategy,"[6] developed by David Ramsey in *The Total Money Makeover*, is a great method and one you should consider if you're overwhelmed by bills and mounting debt.

If your debt-to-income ratio is greater than 45 percent, you need to focus on reducing that percentage. Banks will look at your application more favorably if you can show a history of paying debts. The idea is to be financially stable before buying your home. Lenders don't want to see that your mortgage payments will put you in financial instability. If paying off debt isn't helping your credit score, find a lender who practices manual underwriting. This lender can help you get a mortgage without relying on a credit score. Additionally, if you can put 20 percent down to avoid PMI, do it!

Government-Insured Mortgages

Uncle Sam loves when people buy homes. The United States government benefits from people purchas-

---

6   Dave Ramsey, *The Total Money Makeover: a Proven Plan for Financial Fitness* (Nashville, TN: Thomas Nelson, Inc., 2013).

ing properties and therefore incentivizes it. In addition to the numerous tax benefits, there are also three government institutions that back home loans. Those agencies are the Federal Housing Administration (FHA), the US Department of Agriculture (USDA), and the US Department of Veterans Affairs (VA).

FHA Loans

The Federal Housing Administration provides prospective buyers without a 20 percent down payment and with less than perfect credit the opportunity to become homeowners. With a credit score of 580 or above, FHA loans allow you to put down as little as 3.5 percent. In the event your credit score is under 580, you can still qualify for an FHA loan, but you must put down at least 10 percent and have a credit score over 500. However, putting down less than 10 percent isn't always a bad thing. If a borrower's down payment is less than 10 percent, FHA loans stipulate that they must obtain two mortgage insurance premiums, the first due before closing on the property and the second an annual payment that lasts for the life of the loan.

VA Loans

Veterans of the United States military and their immediate family members can acquire loans backed by the VA. This type of loan represents an incredibly flexible, low-interest rate option that many veterans can take advantage of. The biggest advantages of a VA loan are its low down payment, lack of PMI, and capped closing costs. VA loan borrowers will need to cover a funding fee, which is a set percentage of the loan amount. The funding fee and other minimized closing costs can all be taken care of up front or included on the back end of your loan.

USDA Loans

Do you live in a rural area? Is your county's or town's population less than 10,000? If so, you may be interested in a USDA loan. The USDA provides loans to low-income individuals seeking to purchase a home in a rural area. In order to qualify, your home must be located in a USDA-eligible area. According to the guidelines set by the USDA, an area is considered rural if the population is less than 10,000. Additionally, your income must be under a certain limit to be eligible for the loan. You may or may not be required to pay a down payment for a USDA loan. This varies from region to region. If you meet the location and income requirements, USDA loans are a great way to find mortgage credit in areas where a lack of opportunity exists.

Advantages of Government-Insured Loans

- FICO score minimums aren't as high as conventional limits.
- Down payments are often lower, allowing individuals with small down payments the ability to purchase.
- Both first-time buyers and repeat homeowners can qualify.

Disadvantages of Government-Insured Loans

- Qualification requirements are stringent.
- Obligatory mortgage insurance premiums are unavoidable.
- The costs of closing the loan may be higher than conventional loans.
- The documentation process can be rigorous.

Who Should Get a Government-Insured Loan?

Securing a mortgage backed by the federal government can feel like a lifesaver. The favorable terms make the process much easier than conventional loans. If you don't have a large amount of cash saved or suffer from credit blemishes, consider a government loan. Out of all the various types, VA loans are the most borrower-friendly and are used as an advantage or selling point for recruiters in the military. Even so, USDA loans and FHA loans offer the rest of the population a great alternative to the stricter requirements that come along with conventional loans.

Adjustable-Rate Mortgages

How is the market performing? What are interest rates like? Do you feel like you can pay off the loan before the market shifts? These are all questions you'll want to consider before getting into an adjustable-rate mortgage. As its name makes clear, ARMs have a shifting interest rate that adjusts itself according to the market. Typically, lenders offer ARMs with a fixed rate for the first twelve or twenty-four months that is lower than a conventional loan. Be careful not to fall for this so-called "teaser rate," because after the specified period the loan will adjust itself according to the market for the remainder of the term. You want to be mindful and secure an ARM that has a limit or cap on how much the interest rate or mortgage payment can increase. The last thing you want to see is your payment go from $1,200 to $2,500 overnight.

Advantages of Adjustable-Rate Mortgages
- The first few years of your ARM may lock you in with a lower rate than a conventional loan.
- It is possible to significantly cut down your interest payments with an ARM.

Disadvantages of Adjustable-Rate Mortgages
- There is the possibility that your monthly mortgage jumps up to an unmanageable amount.
- ARMs have high loan-default rates.
- Your financial freedom may be tied to how stable the market is.

Who Should Get an Adjustable-Rate Mortgage?
Typically, buyers that feel extremely confident in their ability to pay off the adjustable-rate mortgage before it adjusts should get one. My personal recommendation is to avoid an ARM at all costs. You never know what circumstances you will run into or what will happen to the economy, and a major shift in the market can affect your monthly payments. This is the reason ARMs have a higher than average default rate.

Sharia-Compliant Mortgages

While they are the norm in some other countries, sharia-compliant mortgages, which follow Islamic financing principles, are becoming more common in the United States among people of all faiths. According to Ibrahim Warde, a professor at Tufts University, "Islamic bank capital has grown from $200 billion in 2000 to close to $3 trillion in 2016."[7]

In a sharia-compliant mortgage, the bank or financial institution will purchase the property with you and lease their proportionate share of a property to you, in return for agreed-upon fixed monthly rental payments. The right of ownership of the asset or the property is transferred to you at the end of the leasing period which, like conventional mortgages, can be fifteen-year or thirty-year terms.

Advantages of Sharia-Compliant Mortgages

- Since the bank is a "co-owner," they share the risk with the homebuyer in the event of a natural disaster or foreclosure.
- There are no prepayment penalties.
- Late payment fees are capped to administrative costs only.
- Since the bank is a co-owner, they set up a nonrecourse commitment, meaning they cannot pursue a buyer's other assets.

---

7 Riyadh Mohammed, "Hot Trend in 2017: Rise of Islamic Banks on Main St. USA," CNBC, December 5, 2016, https://www.cnbc.com/2016/12/02/under-the-radar-islamic-banks-rise-in-th.html.

Disadvantages of Sharia-Compliant Mortgages

- It may be difficult to get approved for a sharia-compliant loan.
- Monthly payments are usually slightly higher each month compared to a conventional mortgage.
- They typically require a minimum 20 percent down payment.

Who Should Get a Sharia-Compliant Mortgage?

Individuals who are looking for extra security by having a partner rather than a typical lender. Additionally, this is a great option for individuals looking to avoid interest, or *riba,* and take on a rent-to-own approach. If you are considering a sharia-complaint mortgage, you may be able to work with a national bank or speak to specialty firms like UIF Corporation or Guidance Residential.

Online Calculator

Regardless of the loan you choose, you can use an online calculator to help you estimate your mortgage payment. I recommend visiting Zillow.com/Mortgage-Calculator or MortgageCalculator.org. Make sure you have the following information on hand:

- down payment
- HOA fees
- home insurance
- interest rate
- PMI
- purchase price
- real estate tax

I also always recommend verifying there are no prepayment penalties, so that you are able to pay off your loan in the future without getting stuck paying additional fees.

Step 5: Talk to a Certified Financial Adviser and Loan Officer

Talking to a certified financial adviser and loan officer will help bring to your attention the details you're over-looking. Be honest regarding your financial health and provide accurate financial documents, such as bank statements, tax returns, bills, etc. to your financial adviser and loan officer. After reviewing your finances, a good financial adviser will help broaden your knowledge of what you can afford, how much to put down, and what additional fees to expect when buying your home. Your loan officer will be a great resource when trying to make important financial decisions regarding your loan and let you know for what you might pre-qualify. The prequalification is a quick calculation the loan officer will do to give you a sense of the types of loans and the amount you may be approved for based on the high-level information you provide. Understand that this is not a commitment and is for informational purposes only.

The next step is to get preapproved for a loan. The preapproval process requires you to complete an application that gives the lender a better understanding of your financial health as well as verify some information via a background check or credit check. If everything checks out with the application, they will be able to provide you preliminary financing approval, as well as an expectation of what rate you can expect. This will be your preapproval letter when submitting an offer on a home. Although the preapproval letter is not a binding commitment, it is typically good for a minimum of ninety days and a maximum of 180 days so that you don't need to complete another application or background check or credit check in that time frame.

Chapter 3:

Finding Your Home

There's no place like home.
— Dorothy, *The Wizard of Oz*

You've probably heard the saying, "home is where the heart is." Home is where you spend most of your time, where you feel comfortable letting your guard down and relaxing, where you unwind after a long, stressful day and spend time with your family or loved ones. A home serves many crucial purposes, so it's important that you find the most fitting home for yourself. Performing proper due diligence on a property before buying is more of an obligation than a recommendation. In this chapter, we'll discuss some critical considerations you must not overlook when securing your home purchase.

Step 1: Interviewing Real Estate Agents

Interviewing and picking the best real estate agent is one of the most important steps you can take before your home search process. Amid the excitement, it can be easy to skip crucial steps needed to secure the perfect home, but there's no reason not to use a real estate agent. They provide vital feedback and guidance throughout the home search. The seller typically pays the commission for both the buyer's and seller's agent, but if you're in a market where the seller does not pay the buyer broker commission, it's still a good idea to hire an agent of your own.

Generally speaking, you won't have to pay a single cent to have an agent help you find the perfect house. Why not have someone knowledgeable in the real estate market advise you, free of charge? Buying a home is the most expensive financial commitment most people make. Ensuring you receive the best advice and counseling possible is critical. Just because you aren't paying the agent directly, however, doesn't mean you should settle for anyone. Countless times, I've seen agents push their clients to sell or buy a home just to make a commission. I've seen professionals willing to invest their hard-earned millions in an expensive home seek the advice of agents with almost zero experience or credibility.

Don't choose an agent simply because he or she is a family friend. Interview several agents and pick the one that's most knowledgeable about the location, price range, style, etc. of the type of home for which you're looking. Ask to see a portfolio of what they've bought and sold. Make sure you're picking the right agent, and don't settle! Here's a list of attributes you should seek in a great agent:

- **Knowledgeable**

  As they say, knowledge is power. If an agent is knowledgeable, they'll most likely have plenty of resources at their disposal to help you. If your agent has it all but isn't knowledgeable about real estate, they won't make a competent adviser. Your agent should be able to speak to all facets of the home buying process. These are a few areas in which your agent should be an expert:

  - **Market Conditions**

    Look for an agent who is active in the market. Someone who is regularly buying and selling for clients would be ideal. This type of agent will have his or her finger on the beating pulse of the market. Like anything else, trends come and go. Understanding where the market is currently at will help you buy smarter.

  - **Location**

    Location. Location. Location. You want to select an agent that understands the local community they serve. And I don't just mean knowing where the good restaurants and local gyms are. The agent you pick should be familiar with the location in which you want to live. If you want to live in Zone A and your agent is only familiar with Zones B and C, they won't be of much help. You want that expert touch of familiarity, local knowledge, and reputability. That's a real estate agent you want to work with.

- **Real Estate Type**

  Agents typically stick to a specific home style or type. Some specialize in million-dollar mansions, some focus on parcels of land or lots, others specialize in farms and ranches, and the list goes on. Make sure your agent is familiar with the home type(s) into which you're looking. If you're trying to find an affordable townhome, you don't want to work with an agent whose portfolio is filled with luxury high-rise condos. Keep that in mind while on the hunt for an agent.

- **Construction and Materials**

  An agent that understands the quality and variety of construction materials will help you acquire the perfect home. Being able to take a look at a house's age, materials, and design, and immediately know its long-term value takes experience. A great agent will be able to point out how well or poorly constructed a property is. This will also help you better understand your long-term maintenance costs.

- **Real Estate Law and Contracts**

  Agents aren't lawyers, but it helps to have an agent who can guide you through a contract and explain some key elements you may need to know. Real estate law and contracts can get complicated. With complicated financing terms, numerous parties, strict closing requirements, and other variables, you need someone who can explain it all in layman's terms. Your agent will review those complicated terms and articulate them in a way that's clear and concise for you.

- **Contingencies**

  A contingency clause can help protect the buyer in the event an item in the contract is not satisfactorily fulfilled. For example, a financing contingency gives the buyer an out if they're not able to ensure the funds for closing. Working out the details of your contingency will be left up to a savvy agent. It's a prudent move that may provide a saving grace at the end of the day.

- **Mortgage**

  Hopefully, you have a reliable mortgage broker that can guide you through the various options to guarantee that you obtain the best rate and loan setup. Having a second pair of eyes doesn't hurt, though. If you can't find a decent loan officer, your agent should be able to direct you to one.

- **Settlement**

  Yes, you should have a settlement agent. However, your real estate agent is the one who should be looking out for your best interests. Ideally, your agent will review your settlement statement and catch any discrepancies or mistakes. Additionally, having your agent walk through everything you sign at closing should help put you at ease.

- **Honesty**

Honesty is crucial. Seek an agent who's dedicated to protecting your best interests. Buying a home can be a very emotional decision. Having an agent ready to expose potential problems is critical. Whether it be financial, market-based, or regarding the house itself, a good agent will help you navigate common pitfalls. Over the years, I've walked away from deals that could have made me hundreds of thousands of dollars because they weren't right for my client. Keeping a client's information confidential and putting a client's interests before their own is a real estate agent's fiduciary responsibility.

- **Effective Communication Skills**

The most significant issue most buyers and sellers face with their real estate agents is the lack of communication. Real estate is a time-sensitive market. You need an agent who can effectively and consistently articulate information. Communication is a two-way street, however, so make sure the agent is a good listener and understands what you're looking for in a home. On day one of meeting with your agent, make a list of "must-haves" and "wants" so the agent can tailor their search appropriately. If you explicitly state, "I need a two-car garage," and your agent keeps sending you one car garage homes, you have a problem. It could be that a two-car garage home is out of your price range, but if you drive out the extra mile, you'll find plenty of two-car garage homes. Be clear about your expectations.

- **References**
  If you're like me, you'll check the Yelp reviews for any new restaurant you want to try, or the Rotten Tomatoes reviews for any new movie you want to see. What about checking how many stars that double-sided tape has on Amazon? We are continuously checking out and leaving reviews on the smallest of purchases. Why not get a reference on your real estate agent too? If they have an online presence, read their reviews. Ask the agent for references for the past five sales they've made. This will help you determine if you're talking to the right agent whose skills are tailored to your needs.

Once you have selected an agent you are comfortable with, you'll sign a buyer broker and agency agreement, which validates the relationship and establishes the agent's fiduciary responsibility to you as the buyer. You can sign an exclusive agreement that obligates you to use that agent exclusively. The advantage of having an exclusive agreement is showing the agent you are serious and committed to them. They'll be more attentive to your wants and make sure information is consistent. A nonexclusive agency allows you to work with any and all agents. The upside of a nonexclusive agreement is that you may receive information and listings from several agents. Exclusive or not, make sure your agreement has a termination option for any reason, so that you're not stuck with an agent you don't like for several months.

Step 2: Searching Within Your Budget

Save time by narrowing your search to homes that fit your financial criteria. Make it a point to stick to the budget. Being realistic with what you can afford, where you are in life, and what you need is crucial. We all want a pool, extra space, and the dream backyard. The "more is better" philosophy runs deep within our society, and we may feel social pressures to purchase items we cannot afford, but this mentality causes many to accumulate vast amounts of debt. By following the steps in this chapter, you'll be able to determine what you can afford. Look for homes that fit your financial needs instead of trying to tailor your financials to match the home you want. Filter out properties outside of your price range. You'll save a lot of time, effort, and heartache by staying within your budget.

Step 3: Previewing Properties Online

We live in a time where almost everything we want is just a click away, including property searches. After a few searches, filters, and clicks, you'll be able to find every single home in the location, price range, and criteria you've specified. You can use sites like Zillow, Redfin, or ZipRealty, to name a few, to give you an idea of the estimated value, market trends, and neighborhood details of your potential home. These tools help consolidate what's in the market that might be of interest to you. Viewing photos and taking virtual tours will assist you in identifying what your preferences are. While these tools are useful, however, they're not always accurate. If you read the fine print, these sites often provide a disclaimer: "Information on this site does not, and the services are not intended to, provide financial or real estate advice and may not be accurate." They also may not take into account the specific terms the sellers are willing to offer or renovations that may have added significant value to the property.

Occasionally, clients send me glitzy-looking condos in their price range and ask for my opinion. Almost always, I'll look at the website description and find that it's missing a condo association fee, which pushes the property outside the monthly payment within the client's budget. Sometimes, a brand-new home will show a price drop of $50,000 online, and eager home buyers are quick to jump at this "opportunity." "No, I'm sorry," I say, "the listing is just pulling the same address for both the 2,400 square foot unit and the 3,200 square foot unit the builder is selling." Do your research and send properties you like to your agent to get their feedback. Let them review all the information and verify whether it's a good fit. Make sure your agent can validate important information like HOA fees, taxes, restrictions, etc. Understand the full picture, and don't jump to conclusions.

I recently had a client who asked me to list their townhome for sale. After researching the market and walking through their twenty-year-old home, I told them they'd get the most value if they were willing to do some slight renovations for $15,000. Otherwise, I expected it would sell for $360,000. They told me my information must be wrong because the neighbors had their townhome listed for $399,990. I took them over to see their neighbors' fully renovated home with brand-new stainless-steel kitchen appliances, granite countertops, and hardwood floors. It was impeccable. They immediately understood what I meant and renovated their home over the next month for just under $15,000. Their home sold for $405,000 three days later. Previewing properties online can be very helpful, but a good real estate agent will be able to see past the clickbait and find the truth for you.

Step 4: Visiting Preselected Properties in Person

All right, you've chosen three to five properties that fit your needs and are within your budget. Now it's time to go take a closer look. First of all, never *ever* purchase a property without viewing it in person. If a picture is worth a thousand words, then seeing something in person is worth a thousand pictures. It is absolutely critical.

No two homes are the same. Every single home is unique, even if they're in the same community and have the same layout. Buying a home is unlike any other purchase you'll make. Let's take buying a new car as an example. You could be living in Virginia but find a new or used car at a dealer in California that you want to purchase. It would make total sense to visit your local dealership and test drive the same vehicle. You can get a list of all the options from the Vehicle Identification Number (VIN) on the California vehicle and test those options at the local Virginia dealership. If the car's right for you, just call the dealer in California and purchase the vehicle, knowing you'll have a full factory warranty on defective parts. The risk is minimal.

Buying a home is much different than buying a car, however. There's probably no home built to the exact same specifications as yours—maybe a similar floor plan, but the property's location, options, materials, and finishes will be vastly different. When I say location, I don't just mean miles apart. Even homes in the same neighborhood won't be identical. One home could be facing the south with all the windows on the north side. Good luck getting any natural light in there. Another home could be right off the street with the sounds and sights of cars passing by the living room every two seconds. But maybe the third home is perfect for you.

This is why viewing a home in person is essential. After all, you will spend a considerable amount of time over the next few years in it. Pictures won't be accurate in depicting the property's dimensions, size, layout, or surroundings. You really need to get a feel for the home, and the only way to do that is to visit in person.

Once you've found the house you want to call home, it's time to make an intelligent and informed offer. And to make an intelligent and informed offer, you need to do your research. Check out the sales price on comparable properties in the neighborhood over the past year. What pros and cons does your potential home have compared to those that have recently sold? How many days has the home been on the market? What's the pricing history? In the next chapter, we'll discuss how you can get comfortable with all the facts before submitting an offer.

Chapter 4:

Making an Offer

Let us never negotiate out of fear. But let us never fear to negotiate.

—John F. Kennedy

Now that you've found a home you like, it's time to put in an offer. Hopefully, in a few short weeks, you'll be lounging in your new living room, reflecting on this whole process. But before you can do that, you must negotiate the best deal possible, which includes much more than the best purchase price. Your offer must be well-informed, so you can back up your negotiation points and be aware of what's going on.

Making a good offer is about finding that sweet spot between balancing your budget, getting the most bang for your buck, and submitting an offer the seller is willing to accept. You also need to be mindful of timing, financing, added costs, etc. As stated in a recent Zillow report, approximately 15 percent of homeowners said that it was challenging to have the seller accept their initial offer on the home they were interested in.[8] There is a lot to consider, but getting your offer accepted can be easily accomplished if you consider and answer the following important questions:

- What's the seller's list price? What incentives are the sellers offering?
- How much can you afford for your monthly payment? (Refer to Chapter 2)
- How much are the extra costs? What do they cover? (Refer to Chapter 2)
- How much additional work does the home require?
- What's your time frame? What's the seller's timeline?
- What's the market value?
- How are market conditions now?
- How competitive is the submarket? Is it a buyer's or seller's market?
- What are the home's features?

Step 1: Considering Home Features

The home's features, options, and amenities will help you assess the value of the home. These features and statistics include items such as:

---

8 "How to Make an Offer on a House," Home Buyers Guide, Zillow, accessed December 20, 2019, https://www.zillow.com/home-buying-guide/making-an-offer-on-a-house/.

- **Home Size**
  What's the home's square footage?
- **Home Type**
  Home types include condominium, townhouse, single-family, etc. Certain home types, such as condos, may come with additional restrictions or costs, such as condo dues or a homeowner association fees.
- **Interior Features**
  Are the appliances included? What about the blinds? This also includes other supplemental features you may be interested in, such as fireplaces, tubs, light fixtures, upgraded cabinets, or quartz versus granite or laminate countertops. Are the floors hardwood, tile, vinyl, or carpet? Is there anything that needs immediate attention? Are there any additional purchases you'll have to make? These are all minor costs that can quickly add up.
- **Lot Size**
  How much land does the home have? Are there any restrictions or easements? A simple title survey should give you all the information you need.
- **Number of Bathrooms**
  Consider the number of full and half baths. Don't confuse a washroom for a full bathroom. If it doesn't include a shower or bathtub, it's considered a half bath.
- **Number of Bedrooms**
  How many bedrooms are in the property, and

how many can be built out if needed? To be considered a bedroom, you need to have a window, closet, and smoke detector installed.

- **Parking**

  Is there a garage or number of assigned spaces? Is there public parking for you or your guests? Is the driveway space adequate for your family?

- **Utilities**

  Who pays for heating, cooling, gas, and electric, you or the HOA? Don't make an offer before getting a sense of what utilities will cost you. Properties that don't have public utilities such as natural gas or public water and sewer can have higher maintenance or usage costs than the average home.

- **Year Built**

  It's crucial to identify what year your potential home was built. The older a home is, the more maintenance it will probably require. Staying on top of those repairs will save you money in the long run. Additionally, wear and tear items like heating or air-conditioning units, windows, roofs, etc. typically don't add value to the home when replaced but rather keep it up to par with market standards. Keep that in mind when a seller starts explaining all the items that have been recently renovated.

Step 2: Creating a Comparative Market Analysis

Once you have answered these questions, you will be able to consider the total cost of homeownership and make a well-thought-out offer. A great way to efficiently answer these questions is by creating a property information sheet, which includes the seller's list price, incentives, home features, and the extra costs associated with the property. Any information you don't have on hand can be found on the listing or in public records, and when in doubt, always ask your agent so they can help gather this information.

To take it a step further, ask your agent to also create a Comparative Market Analysis (CMA). A CMA is a helpful way to understand the home's market value and current market conditions. As mentioned before, no two homes are exactly alike; therefore, it's incredibly difficult to utilize an apples-to-apples approach when trying to find your future home's market value. It's crucial to analyze the details of similar properties to make a quantitative assumption on your potential homes value. Below, are a few metrics you should take into consideration:

- **Days on Market (DOM)**
  How many days has this home been on the market? How many days, on average, are homes in the community on the market? The amount of days a house has been on the market is a significant statistic to know. Most prospective buyers, realtors, and even real estate investors

will associate a house with a high DOM as being undesirable. There must be a reason the house isn't selling, right? Some buyers may think the house has costly issues that need to be repaired. It could just be that the price point is too high. A smart buyer will leverage this and negotiate the best price possible. If a home has been on the market for a significant period of time, the seller will be more receptive to negotiations. Sometimes the motivation to sell is enough to save you thousands of dollars. Sellers are usually selling in order to move on to a new chapter of their lives and are probably aiming to sell by a specific date. If the home is vacant, they'll have carrying costs such as a mortgage, utilities, etc. that accrue daily. The longer the house is on the market, the more likely you'll be able to negotiate a better price.

- **List Price versus Sold Price**
Since you've compiled a list of homes that have sold in the past twelve months, it's time to use it. A good exercise in making a strong offer is checking both the listed price and the final selling price. This useful statistic will help you understand how much room you have to negotiate and how to make a firm offer.

- **Price per Square Foot**
Homes situated in a community or general vicinity can vary in price and size. As you probably know, size can especially impact the price of a home. A good way to decipher the proper-

ty value is to look at the price per square foot. As an example, Home A is 2,500 square feet and sold for $350,000, while Home B is a 2,800 square foot home and sold for $385,000. To figure out the price per square foot, you'd use the following formula: price per square foot = sales price / home size. In the case of Home A, $350,000 / 2,500 = $140.00. As for Home B, $385,000 / 2,800 = $137.50. Based on this simple two home scenario, you can infer that the house you're looking at should be priced between $137.50–$140.00 per square foot.

- **Similar Homes for Sale**
  What are homes in the neighborhood, city, or county selling for? How many houses are for sale? As an example, if there are two new townhomes in a five-mile radius priced under $400,000, the demand may outweigh the supply, and therefore, you need to move quickly. However, if there are eighty new townhomes in the same area, you would have more buying power and be able to be more selective or offer a lower price. Consider how competitive the home is priced based on the home's features compared with other available homes on the market.

- **Similar Homes That Have Sold**
  In your CMA, you should be able to see a list of all comparable homes that have sold in the past twelve months. Based on those comparisons and sales dates, you may be able to view

specific trends like price increases, fewer days on the market, an increase in the average price per square foot, etc. These trends will help you analyze and determine what your offer should entail.

Now that you've answered all the questions and consulted with your real estate agent, you should have a good idea of the price and terms you're going to offer the seller. At this point, you should have adequately analyzed the home's features, prepared your budget, and considered added costs, and you should feel comfortable with moving forward.

Step 3: Writing Your Purchase and Sale Agreement

The next step is to draft an offer with a written Purchase and Sale Agreement (PSA). The best way to do this is to use your state's standard approved template. State standard templates are a convenient way of guaranteeing you have a comprehensive PSA that includes all state-required legal language and laws. If you draft your own PSA from scratch, you could incure high legal fees as well as potentially miss some critical pieces of information. The standard templates are typically formatted to allow for fill-in-the-blanks answers and have little check mark boxes to select the appropriate conditions behind your transaction. Consult with a local attorney on your PSA. Having them review or fill it in as needed is the optimal choice.

You'll want to make sure you have the following

information completed correctly:

- **Address and Legal Property Description**
The address and legal property description information can be found through your county's public property records. Your agent should be able to provide this information to you as well.

- **Buyer's and Seller's Information**
Names are an obvious necessity. Additionally, having information like forwarding addresses or emails can help you receive crucial documents down the road.

- **Closing Costs Assistance**
This is one point I cannot stress enough: I always recommend that clients ask for a percentage of their offer (2 percent to 4 percent, depending on what your financing lender will allow) in closing cost assistance. Asking for closing costs assistance will ultimately save you from spending money toward closing costs and lets you focus on putting more down toward your principal, thus lowering your interest payments in the long term. My recommendation to buyers is to negotiate this even more than the sales price. Essentially, you're reducing the sale price by 2 percent to 4 percent and saving thousands in interest payments that you would have paid otherwise.

- **Earnest Money Deposit**
An Earnest Money Deposit (EMD), also known as a security deposit, helps to show you're serious about buying the home. Putting down an

EMD that's refundable until contingencies are waived is a great way to prove just how serious you are to a seller. Depending on your market standard, this deposit could be as little as $1,000 or as high as 5 percent of your purchase price.

- **Home Warranty**

  Unless you're buying a brand-new home from a builder, it's a good idea to ask for a home warranty, paid for by the seller for the first year of ownership, as you never know what could come up. The warranty would be provided by a third party and depending on the package chosen, can cover anything from appliances to the homes structure. In the event you are buying new, it might give you some peace of mind to know that builders typically offer a warranty for the first year of ownership. Ask the builder for their specific warranty conditions.

- **Legal Requirements**

  Each state has different legal requirements and disclosures, and real estate law can be extremely technical. Using the most up-to-date, state-approved contract will prevent future issues, especially in the unfortunate circumstance that litigation is necessary.

- **Personal Property and Fixtures**

  Make sure to specify what is being conveyed (appliances, blinds, light fixtures, etc.) with the property. It doesn't hurt to list these items in writing to avoid confusion at closing.

- **Price**

  Specify how much and how you'll be paying for the home, including any amount you plan on borrowing (e.g., 20 percent down with an 80 percent loan).

- **Settlement Agent**

  The buyer gets to select who they want to use as the settlement agent. The settlement agent is basically a middleman who collects funds from the purchaser and ensures the seller pays any outstanding lenders, contractors, taxes, lien holders, etc. before providing you with the property title. For example, your EMD would be sent to the settlement agent, who would hold the funds in an escrow account.

- **Settlement Date**

  The day you plan to close on the property is known as the settlement date. Make sure you allocate enough time to take care of all contingencies outlined below. Typically, the settlement date should be thirty to forty-five days after the contract ratification.

Step 4: Verifying Contingencies

Once all the items above are included in your contact, you'll want to verify that you have the appropriate contingencies and supporting addendums. Our world is filled with an inordinate amount of uncertainty. Similarly, real estate is filled with hypothetical what-ifs that can lead a person down an endless number of rabbit holes. What if the main sewer line you just repaired bursts again? What happens if the seller doesn't want to go through with closing? The bank just delivered a rock bottom appraisal, now what? This list goes on and on. These what-ifs are addressed and covered in what is known as contingency clauses.

A contingency clause is a contract provision in your PSA that requires a specific event or action to take place for the contract to be considered valid. You can consider your contingency clauses as a form of protection to retrieve your EMD in the event closing does not occur for a reason outside of your control. While contingency clauses can help you with any unforeseen circumstances, in a competitive market, they can also hinder your chances of getting a ratified purchase and sale agreement. Consult with your agent on what clauses work best for you.

There are many different types of contingency clauses that can be added to your purchase and sale agreement, and while anything is possible, we'll focus on some of the most common items:

- **Appraisal Contingency**

  Under an appraisal contingency clause, if the home appraises for a significantly lower price than the contract value, the buyer can ask the seller to adjust the sales price so that it aligns with the appraised value or have the option to terminate the purchase and sale agreement with a full refund of the EMD.

- **Financing**

  If your offer is not a cash purchase, you'll need

to make sure your offer is contingent on obtaining financing with a not-to-exceed interest rate clause. This way, you'll cover yourself in the event you cannot obtain financing or interest rates spike, affecting your ability to make monthly payments.

- **Lead-Based Paint**

  If the property was constructed before 1978, there may be a chance it contains lead-based paint, which could be harmful to inhale. According to the Centers for Disease Control, lead-based paint and lead-contaminated dust are the most widespread and hazardous sources of lead exposure. A lead paint inspection tells you the lead content of every painted structural part (doors, walls, windows, etc.) of your home. However, it won't tell you whether the paint is a hazard or how you should deal with it. A risk assessment tells you if there are any severe lead hazards, such as peeling paint and lead dust, and what actions to take to address these hazards. Homes built after 1978 don't necessarily have this issue so a lead-based paint contingency may not be required in that circumstance.

- **Owner Association Docs**

  If the property is part of an HOA or condo association, make sure your contract is contingent on you receiving the relevant documents with enough time to review them thoroughly. Take time to review the HOA documents to make sure there are no additional costs or restrictions on your future home.

- **Property Condition Report**

  Always get a property condition report (PCR) done. A property condition report is completed by a certified inspector who will give you insight on the condition of the property, with critical information such as the remaining life span on existing utilities, roof, and appliances. A certified inspector can find termites, safety hazards, water damage, broken appliances, and so on. This inspection can save you thousands in costly repairs. Most of the time, sellers are willing to fix the issues presented in the PCR or credit you for the damages at settlement. From my experience, the PCR has either saved clients from purchasing a bad property or saved them thousands in repairs. Make sure you work with a certified inspector that has the experience you need in delivering an adequate inspection.

- **Property Sale**

  If this isn't your first home, and you need to sell your current home to buy this property, make sure your PSA is contingent on the sale of your current home. You don't want to lose your EMD in the event your current home doesn't sell.

- **Title**

  A homebuyer can void a purchase contract if a title company reveals an issue that could prevent the buyer from becoming the property's new owner or any findings that affect the property's marketability or use.

- **Wood-Destroying Insect Inspection**
  A pest control inspector can generate a report identifying any potential termites or other insects that could be harmful to the property. Depending on your contingency clause, if any severe infestations are found, the seller will have the option to remedy the situation, offer you a credit for the necessary repairs, or you'll be able to get a refund of your deposit and walk away from the PSA.

Step 5: Submitting Your Offer

Next, submit a personal letter to the sellers with your PSA. This will provide the seller with insight and create a personal connection to help make your offer stand out. With your offer, make sure to also provide the following documents:

- **Copy of the EMD Check**
  Your real estate agent should be able to help you determine a deposit that shows you're serious. As previously mentioned, based on your market, this could be anywhere from $1,000 to 5 percent or the purchase price.
- **Preapproval Letter from Your Lender**
  Keep in mind that the preapproval letter, mentioned in previous chapters, comes from your lender and serves as proof that you qualify for financing up to a certain limit. It will typically

be issued after a lender has had the chance to properly analyze your financial background. This letter will guide you to homes within your price range, while offering you peace of mind that you can afford what you're looking at.

- **PSA on First Home**
  If your offer is contingent on the sale of another property, the seller will likely be more comfortable accepting this contingency by showing them a ratified PSA, or at least proof that your first home is already listed and on the market.

Once you've submitted an offer, your seller has two choices, either accept your offer or counter with changes to terms or price. Zillow research shows that just under half of buyers have their first offer accepted. According to the report, 25 percent of buyers make two offers, and 20 percent make three or more until they agree on terms.[9] If the seller counters, you'll be able to review the terms and sales price they've adjusted. If they work for you, great! You can accept their offer. If the terms and price don't sit well with you, it's time to counter again until terms are agreed upon. Once the terms of the PSA are accepted and signed by both the buyer and seller, the PSA is considered ratified, and you're officially under contract.

---

9 "How Long Does It Take to Buy a House? 6 Fast Steps," Home Buyers Guide, Zillow, accessed February 8, 2020, https://www.zillow.com/home-buying-guide/how-long-does-it-take-to-buy-a-house/.

Chapter 5:

Post Ratified Contract

Buying a home today is a complex process, but that in no way excuses home buyers from their obligation for due diligence.

—Henry Paulson

You've found your dream home, made an informed offer, and now have a ratified purchase and sale agreement. The time frame between a ratified PSA and closing is when you are able to conduct inspections, appraisals, and make sure the property is in good standing. From this point, you'll typically have thirty to forty-five days, as outlined in your PSA, to fulfill your purchase contract.

Step 1: Mark Your Calendar

The first step is to make a list of all the key dates set

in the PSA, so you don't miss anything. Take into consideration your contingencies along with their deadline dates, which depend on the allotted time frame specified in your contract. Using a calendar or a planner can be a helpful way to stay on top of important deadlines and keep yourself organized.

Step 2: Deposit Your Earnest Money Deposit

Your EMD, along with a copy of the ratified PSA, should be mailed out to your title company as soon as possible. Your EMD proves to the seller that you'll carry out the transaction in good faith. Failure to deliver the EMD within the time frame allotted in the PSA may result in a breach of the PSA and nullify the agreement.

Step 3: Communicate with Your Lender Immediately

Send your lender a copy of the ratified PSA and ask them what documents they need to get you approved for your loan. Your lender will send a list of documents and information required to get you fully approved and cleared to close. Be proactive, and make sure to provide this information to your lender in a timely fashion. Some of these documents may include:
- bank statements
- driver's licenses
- most recent pay stubs
- payments with associated debt

- tax returns from the last two to three years
- verification of funds
- W2

Remember, this isn't a comprehensive list, so it's imperative to check with your lender for any additional information that you might need to send along.

In some cases, your lender may give you options on paying a fee to buy down your interest rate or locking your interest rate sixty to ninety days before closing. This may be a good option depending on market expectations so checking with a financial advisor is advisable. If all things are the same my recommendation would be to use those funds to pay down your mortgage which will effectively lower your monthly payment.

Once your loan is approved, your lender will provide you with a closing disclosure (CD). A CD is a document that includes all the borrower's closing costs, as well as loan terms and monthly payments. Regulations require a lender to provide a mortgage borrower with the closing disclosure three business days before the loan closing.

Step 4: Schedule Inspections and Appraisals

If your offer is contingent on any inspections or appraisals, you'll want to schedule them sooner rather than later. Inspectors and appraisers may need some lead time to coordinate with their schedules before the deadline. Your lender will probably want to have a report from an approved appraiser in hand before accepting your loan. That's why it's important to co-ordinate with your lender as well.

Property Inspection

Once your property inspector gets to work, they'll analyze and investigate the entire property from top to bottom. The inspector will be careful to point out any of the major electrical, sewage, and other systems, and take note of where they are located and how they function. They'll also identify issues that stand out or may require long-term maintenance. Overall, the purpose of the inspection is to make sure there are no safety issues or costly repairs associated with the home that you did not know about. You'll also be able to become acquainted with the new home and better understand its components and avoid potential con-cerns. While the inspector is a professional and will go over all items in detail, here are a few items you may want to check out for yourself and ensure are inspected:

- **Appliances**
  Make sure the inspector runs the microwave, dishwasher, stove, etc., to make sure they're in good working order.
- **Electrical Outlets**
  Some inspectors disregard electrical outlets, but checking to make sure each outlet is work-ing is important as repair costs could be hun-dreds of dollars.

- **Heating, Ventilation, and Air Conditioning**

  The heating, ventilation, and air conditioning (HVAC) unit is expensive to replace. Costs could reach about a few thousand dollars, depending on the unit. Make sure the inspector checks the condition as well as the expected remaining life of the unit.

- **Light Fixtures**

  Turn lights on and make sure they work. If any bulbs are out, you can ask that they are replaced to match the other light bulbs in the fixture or room.

- **Sinks and Faucets**

  Make sure the water pressure is good and that you have both hot and cold water available for each sink, shower, and faucet.

- **Smoke and Carbon Monoxide Detectors**

  A working smoking and carbon monoxide detector could save your life and your home from a catastrophic event. If smoke detectors are not working properly at the time of sale, insurance companies may try to avoid paying deductibles in the event of a disaster.

- **Sump Pump**

  Sump pumps are convenient features for pumping out any standing water that may pool under your house. But if the sump pump is clogged or otherwise nonfunctional, it could cause a lot of expensive damage by backing up or pumping the water somewhere it shouldn't be going.

- **Toilets**

Flush each toilet in the home just to make sure it works. You don't want to find out a toilet doesn't flush after closing!

- **Water Damage**

  Be mindful of completing a visual inspection to look for water damage at the baseboards, ceilings, and floors.

- **Water Heater**

  Make sure the inspector checks the water heater and ensures it's working correctly. Knowing the remaining life of the unit is a plus as well.

- **Windows**

  Open and close every single window to confirm latches are not broken.

The inspector will document all their findings and send them to you in a comprehensive report. After you have ensured there are no significant issues, and the deal is done, you'll want to keep in mind where everything in the home is and start to formulate plans for both short-term and long-term maintenance.

Property Appraisal

A property appraiser is a bit different from the property inspector. Appraisers estimate the value of a property and are typically called in to appraise the home before the final sale. The appraiser will analyze the property and compare it to similar homes. He or she will note the unique attributes of both the property and the surrounding area. For example, your appraiser may take note of a busy highway nearby, the condition of the roof, or other renovation projects. The appraiser will photograph the building's exterior and rooms in order to document the condition of the property. Afterward, the appraiser will carefully consider the data to provide you with an accurate justification of the home's value, based on the home's condition and market comparables.

Step 5: Review Inspection and Appraisal Reports

Once you have the PCR and appraisal back from the inspector and appraiser, you'll have the opportunity to negotiate any potential repairs with the seller. Some sellers are willing to cover the repairs, while others may provide a financial concession to waive the contingency. Some sellers may refuse to make any repairs nor provide any concessions. At this point, you'll need to consider the number of required repairs and the costs associated with reaching a reasonable conclusion with the seller. It's always a good idea to ask for your agent's opinion and figure out what's customary in the market for any of the applicable items as well.

Step 6: Obtain Home Insurance

Make sure you get the correct insurance and coverage needed. Have an insurance agent help you find the best rate and coverage plan, considering your home's specific needs. Your insurance coverage should start the day you close.

Mortgage lenders often require each buyer to procure home insurance to help secure their purchase; thus, many home insurance policies can be combined with your monthly mortgage payment and real estate taxes to create a single lump sum due every month. However, some insurance policies might need to be paid for separately, so check with your agent on payment plans and options for your specific situation.

One of the great things about a home insurance policy is that homeowners can select a plan that fits their unique budget. One way of reducing or increasing the cost of your insurance is by adding a deductible. A higher deductible will typically result in a lower cost insurance plan. However, be cognizant of weighing the pros and cons before you choose to add a deductible. In the case of an emergency, these deductibles will require out-of-pocket costs to the homeowner. Be conservative in selecting a deductible that fits your budget and addresses all your needs.

Keep in mind that a homeowner's insurance policy does not typically cover earthquake and flood damage. If you live in an area prone to these natural disasters, it's advisable to include insurance to safeguard your home from these types of catastrophes. Additionally, the Insurance Information Institute warns that disasters such as floods, earthquakes, and hail may require different deductibles. Be very clear on what is and isn't covered in your home insurance policy so there are no surprises.

Step 7: Turn on the Utilities

With all the moving parts involved in purchasing a home, this one is always forgotten. Make sure to call the appropriate utility companies before closing and have them register the utilities under your name as of the day of closing.

Step 8: Update HOA and Inform Service Contractors

If the property is located under an HOA, make sure they have your information on file along with the closing date. This way, you'll get letters, bills, and notices sent to you. If there are any contractors providing services for the property, make sure they're also aware of your new ownership start date and inform them of any services you may not want to continue. A few examples of these service contractors may include:
- home security monitoring
- landscaping contractors
- pest control companies
- swimming pool maintenance companies

If you've done your due diligence and are comfortable with the property inspection report, your appraisal report came in at the same price or higher than your purchase price, you've secured your loan and all contingencies have been waived, then you can move forward with closing. I recommend submitting an addendum to the purchase and sale agreement removing all contingencies and stating that you are moving forward with the purchase of your new home.

Chapter 6:

Closing

Buy land; they're not making any more of it.
—Mark Twain

We're in the home stretch now (pun intended). Closing is the process of finalizing the sale, signing the last set of documents, and transferring the remainder of the funds to the seller. The closing process wraps up when the deed is recorded. As soon as that happens, the home is officially yours!

Closing isn't handled directly by the buyer and seller but rather by a neutral agent. Often, closing is done by a title company that the buyer and seller have agreed upon in advance. Most title companies will also handle the escrow (in some cases, it's a real estate attorney). There are several prerequisites to closing a property sale, and the closing agent's job is to ensure all are executed properly. The three most important requirements for closing are the following:

- the buyer signs the deed of trust for the mortgage (if applicable)
- the sale funds are transferred to the seller
- the title to the property is transferred from the seller to the buyer

Remember, the sale proceeds are not the only item of monetary value exchanged during closing. Depending on how the sale contract was set up, there will probably be other fees as well, such as property taxes, commission(s) to the realtor(s), or title insurance. As the buyer, you must accomplish four key items for the property sale to close:

Step 1: Perform a Final Walk-through Inspection

You have the option to complete a final walk-through of the property before the sale closes. This is typically done within twenty-four hours of the scheduled closing time. Think of it as your last chance to make sure everything in the house meets your expectations and matches what was agreed upon in the purchase and sale agreement. This is your opportunity to ensure that any repairs you may have requested were completed, that any appliances or furniture that were supposed to be included are still there, and so on. Once the sale closes, you won't be able to request any of these items from the seller, so it's crucial that you're sure everything is as it should be during this step. If something is missing or some of the repairs were not completed, don't worry; the escrow agent can hold a commensurate portion of money in escrow to ensure the items are resolved after closing.

Step 2: Decide How You Want to Take Title to the Property

Defining the type of title you're acquiring is important because it determines the legal status of your ownership. This can have consequences down the line that will affect how the property can be transferred, what happens to the property if you or a co-owner pass away, and how the property might be passed down. Depending on what state you're in, there may be specific laws restricting how you can hold the title, and in some states, there are even laws that can change the title, depending on what you do after you've taken ownership. Different states also have different laws regulating how property is taxed, which can vary based on how it is titled. It is a good idea to consult with a lawyer, your realtor, or your title company to guarantee you understand how your title choice will affect your property. To help you get a general sense of the different types of titles, here are a few examples:

- **Sole Title (or Fee Simple Absolute Title)**
  If you hold fee simple absolute title, that means you, and you alone, are the owner of the property. This gives you the full powers, privileges, and liabilities available to a property owner under the law. If you're married, but have decid-

ed to claim the sole title, your deed will reflect that. As an example, your deed may say, "John Doe, a married man, takes possession as his sole and separate property." Be aware that in some states, like California, this titling may not be permanent. In such so-called "community property states," the law stipulates that if an individual takes sole title but uses a bank account shared with a spouse to pay the mortgage and other property expenses, then over time the law will recognize the title as a joint tenancy instead of sole title. Consult with a real estate attorney regarding the specifics of your property and state laws.

- **Joint Tenancy with Right of Survivorship**
This is the most common form of tenancy for married couples, and in most states, the title will default to this form if the purchasers of a property are married. Joint tenancy conveys an equal interest in a piece of real property to each of the parties involved. The distinguishing factor of joint tenancy with the right of survivorship is that if one party passes away, the title transfers to the survivor(s) in equal proportion. This rule applies whether or not the decedent has a valid will and overrides any contrary provisions that may be in the decedent's will. Joint tenancy requires four "unities" under the law:
    - interest, which means each party enjoys the same, equal share of ownership
    - possession, which means each party en-

joys the same right of use or possession of the property
- time, which means each party must acquire title simultaneously
- title, which means each party must acquire title in the same deed or other title documents

If one of the joint tenants sells or otherwise transfers his/her interest to an individual who was not part of the original joint tenancy, this dissolves the joint tenancy and automatically creates a "tenancy in common." In some states, you may find that joint tenancy is referred to as "tenancy by the entirety." In practice, this is the same as joint tenancy, but the owners must be married. In joint tenancy, there is no such requirement.

- **Tenancy in Common**
  Think of tenancy in common as a more flexible version of joint tenancy. Tenants in common share equal rights to use and possession of the property and are not allowed to exclude any of the other tenants in common from using or possessing it. However, this doesn't mean they have to pay into the property equally or own equal shares of the property. Responsibility for costs like property taxes or repairs is proportional to the ownership share.
- **Corporations, Partnerships, and Trusts**
  It is important to know that titles can be vested in a corporation, partnership, or trust, and do

not have to be vested in an individual. Since the law recognizes them as legal entities, distinct from the individuals that comprise them, corporations, partnerships, and trusts can have special tax and probate consequences or benefits. Consult with a licensed real estate or estate planning attorney if this is something in which you are interested.

In addition to selecting how you want to acquire the title, it's imperative to confirm that your title is protected. Title insurance safeguards home buyers and mortgage lenders against deficiencies or issues with a property's title when there is a transfer of property ownership. If a title dispute arises during a sale, the title insurance company may be responsible for paying specific legal damages, depending on the policy. My recommendation is to always get a title insurance policy, it's a onetime cost that helps prevent any potential issues down the road.

Step 3: Sign the Closing Documents

When signing the closing documents, reading the fine print is critical. You will receive a lot of long-winded documents full of legalese, so you may want to consider bringing your attorney or realtor to the signing to verify you understand all the closing documents and their potential implications. Read everything, so you're aware of what you're agreeing to, and double check to catch any errors before the papers are finalized.

The most important document in the closing package will be the settlement statement (sometimes referred to as a HUD-1). You should receive this document, usually labeled "estimated," at least one day before the scheduled closing date. Hopefully, you've received preliminary settlement statements earlier for review, so there are no surprises delaying closing. The settlement statement is like an accounting ledger entry that breaks down all the income (i.e., your down payment, funds from your mortgage lender, any credits you may have received from the seller) and expenses (i.e., closing costs, property taxes, realtor commissions) that will go in and out of escrow. It will also specify the type of loan and loan number (if any), the title/escrow company's file number for this transaction, and the date and location of the settlement. There will be two columns on the settlement statement, one for the seller's debits and credits and one for the buyer's debits and credits. Reading this ledger of income and expenses will help you validate that nothing got left out or double-charged.

At the bottom of the settlement statement, there will be two key line items for you to pay attention to:

- **Gross Amount Due from Borrower (or Buyer)** The gross amount due from borrower (or buyer) is the total amount with all closing costs and fees paid by you, the buyer, for the purchase of your new home. This will include your initial deposit, down payment, and the principal amount of your mortgage (if applicable). This is the amount you'll need to pay into escrow for the sale to close.

- **Gross Amount Due to Seller**

  This is the amount that the seller pockets once the sale has closed. This should equal the sale price minus any existing loans the seller may have (which are typically paid out of escrow) and any settlement charges.

Below is a list of some potential charges you may see in your settlement statement:

- **Appraisal Fee**

  As previously discussed, your lender will ask that you get a certified appraiser to conduct a home inspection. Most appraisers require you to pay this fee before they share the appraisal, but if you didn't pay for this outside of closing, then it'll appear on your settlement statement.

- **Attorney Fees**

  If you haven't paid your real estate attorney outside of the settlement, you could see their fee on the settlement statement.

- **Document Fees**

  The cost for the title company to prepare all the documents you're signing.

- **Escrow Deposit**

  Some lenders will require you to put a couple of months' worth of property taxes, mortgage insurance, and property insurance in an escrow account at closing.

- **Escrow Fees**

The cost for the title company, attorney or escrow agent who's managing the closing on your behalf.

- **Escrow for Miscellaneous Costs**

  Miscellaneous costs will cover any other outstanding costs to be handled outside of closing. These could be items not resolved from the home inspection, utility bills, or other associated charges.

- **Filing Fees**

  The cost to file and record your documents with the city or county.

- **HOA or Condo Setup Fee**

  If your home is in an HOA or condominium association, you may be required to pay an initiation fee to get you set up.

- **Home Inspection Fee**

  Most inspectors require you to pay a home inspection fee before they share their final report, but if you didn't pay for this outside of closing, then you'll find it on your settlement statement.

- **Homeowners Insurance**

  The lender will require you to either pay the first year's insurance up front or set aside the money for first-year payments in the escrow deposit.

- **Title Insurance**

  The cost of the title insurance policy is a one-time payment and covers you as long as you own the home.

Step 4: Transfer the Remainder of Your Down Payment to Escrow

Once you're satisfied with the condition of your property, and you've reviewed the settlement statement, it's time to spend some money. Your initial EMD will be credited toward your down payment. Now, you need to pay the remaining amount of your down payment (or the entire purchase price if you're paying cash) into escrow. If you're financing your purchase with a mortgage, your lender will coordinate with escrow separately to wire them the amount you're borrowing.

Once you've completed all these steps and the funds have transferred through escrow, you have officially completed the purchase of your new property. Congratulations!

Chapter 7:

Post Purchase

There's no place like home.
—John Howard Payne

After successfully becoming a homeowner, there are several important tasks to cross off your checklist. The following is a list I have made over the years covering what I think are the most important things on which you should focus. It'll be broken up into three sections: tasks you should have completed before closing but may have put off until after closing, tasks to complete in the first thirty days of homeownership, and long-term tasks to keep in mind.

Tasks You Should Have Completed Before Closing

Purchase a Home Warranty
Even the most detailed home inspection during a due

diligence period can occasionally miss something. If you didn't buy your new home directly from a builder and a home warranty was not included in your contract with the seller, you may want to consider purchasing a home warranty for at least the first year of your new ownership. The warranty will protect you against any defect you may find that was not revealed during due diligence.

Transfer Your Utilities

Similarly, don't forget to transfer your utility accounts to your new address so you can start living in your new home without any nuisances. For utilities, be sure to transfer the water, gas, and electrical utility services at your new home to your name, or schedule appointments to have these utilities reactivated.

Tasks to Complete in the First Thirty Days After Closing

Setup Internet/Cable/Phone

Contact your internet, phone, and cable providers to set appointments to activate these services at your new home.

Change Your Locks

Changing your locks is like physical insurance for your new home. Even though you'll be getting keys and garage door openers from the seller, there's no way to know who else might have copies. To ensure your privacy and security, you should have all exterior locks—

doors, gates, and garage door openers rekeyed or re-programmed. A new lockset can cost anywhere from $50 to $150. On average, homes have two exterior doors. This means it should only cost around $100 to $300 and a little bit of time to change out the locks and reprogram your garage door(s).

Get a Professional Deep Cleaning

Although it's usually standard practice to clean a home before selling it, you can't be sure how thoroughly it was cleaned. To make sure all the nooks and crannies are free of any leftover dirt and grime, you may want to hire a professional cleaning service to complete a deep clean before you move your belongings into the house. Deep cleaning an empty home typically costs around $200, which is a small price to pay for the convenience and peace of mind that you'll be starting on a clean slate.

Keep a Fire Extinguisher in the Kitchen

According to data from the National Fire Protection Association, based on 2013–2017 annual averages, cooking equipment is the leading cause of home fires and fire injuries, responsible for 49 percent of residential fires.[10] Most fires that occur in the kitchen are grease fires, which can't be put out with water. Keeping a fire extinguisher in the kitchen is an easy and cheap way to safeguard your new home from this po-

10   "Cooking," Public Education, National Fire Protection Association, accessed July 1, 2020, https://www.nfpa.org/Public-Education/Fire-causes-and-risks/Top-fire-causes/Cooking.

tential hazard.

Update Address Information

Buying a home entails a whirlwind of change. As you're moving into your new home, it's important to remember that this is now your new primary address. Be sure to update your contact information to your new address with the state (driver's license, post office, car registration, voter registration, etc.) and any important vendors you do business with (bank, credit cards, etc.). You can also forward any mail from your old address to your new home by completing an online form on the United States Postal Services (USPS) website, USPS.com. Per their site, customers have three mail forwarding options:

- **Temporary Change of Address**

  A temporary change of address order provides for piece-by-piece forwarding of primarily First-Class Mail® service and periodicals for a specified period, but generally does not provide the forwarding of USPS Marketing Mail® or package services mail.

- **Permanent Change of Address**

  A permanent change of address order provides for piece-by-piece forwarding of primarily First-Class Mail® service for twelve months and periodicals for sixty days, but generally does not provide the forwarding of USPS Marketing Mail® service or package services. The customer's new address is provided to business mailers upon request through mailer endorsements on a mail-piece.

- **Premium Forwarding Service Residential®
  Service (PFS-Residential® Service)**
  PFS-Residential® service provides a single weekly shipment of all mail for a residence via Priority Mail® service for a fee. The service can be extended for up to a year. PFS-Residential is temporary and is offered as an additional option to the free temporary or permanent change of address option.[11]

Set Up Your Mortgage and HOA Payments Online

Many homeowners miss setting up their online payment portals for their HOA and mortgage accounts after completing their home purchase. You may not receive any information for a few weeks, but that doesn't mean you're not responsible for the payments. If you don't hear from the HOA or mortgage company, be proactive and reach out so that your first payment isn't late.

Close Out Your Escrow

If you have any outstanding items that weren't resolved at closing, such as an unpaid utility bill from the seller or any outstanding maintenance costs owed by the seller, make sure to follow up and resolve these outstanding issues by closing out your escrow.

---

11   "Mail Forwarding Options," FAQs, United States Postal Service, accessed on August 1, 2020, https://faq.usps.com/s/article/Mail-Forwarding-Options.

Tasks to Complete Long Term

Regularly Maintain Your Home

Just like getting checkups at the doctor, performing regular preventative maintenance on your home can prevent larger problems from appearing later. Address seemingly minor issues immediately, so they don't balloon into expensive or potentially disastrous problems in the future. Here are a few major maintenance tasks for you to monitor:

- **Keep Your HVAC Filters Fresh**

  Your HVAC system has filters to remove dust and harmful particles from the air that get circulated through your home. You should change your filter(s) and install quality replacements at least every three months. This will save you money on heating and cooling costs by keeping your HVAC systems running efficiently and will contribute to the unit's longevity as well. Consider buying the filters in bulk, so you don't have to run to the store for them every three months.

- **Winter-Proof Your Exterior Water Lines**

  This is especially important if you live in a cold climate. Water left in hose bibs or pipes can freeze, and when water freezes, it expands. This expansion can crack your pipes and create a very expensive problem. Each year, before the frost sets in, find the shutoff valve(s) for your hose bib(s), which should be inside your house, and shut them off. Remove any hoses from your outdoor spigots and drain them of any water before you store them.

- **Test Your Sump Pump**

  Sump pumps are convenient features for pumping out any standing water that may pool under your house, but if your sump pump is clogged or otherwise nonfunctional, it could cause a lot of expensive damage by backing up or pumping the water somewhere it shouldn't be going. If you have a sump pump, it's probably located in your basement or crawl space. Make sure to test it regularly to ensure that it is in proper working order.

Find Out If You Qualify for a Government Homestead Exception

Many counties have homestead exceptions that can provide property tax benefits for qualified applicants. These benefits work by reducing the assessed value of your home as recorded by your county tax collector and thereby reducing your property tax bill. Specific requirements vary by county, but most counties will give exceptions to veterans and senior citizens.

Assign a Power of Attorney

Assigning a limited power of attorney to someone you trust will ensure that your home can be effectively managed, rented, or sold in case you're unable to, for any reason.

Execute a Last Will and Testament

Nobody ever wants to think about their last will, but it's crucial in guaranteeing that your most valuable asset is handled the way you want in a worst-case scenario. As discussed in Chapter 6, the way your home is titled may be a major factor in what happens with the asset after your passing. Check your state laws and consult with an attorney on how to best prepare.

Have an Emergency Plan in Place

The best time to respond to an emergency is before it happens. Building a comprehensive emergency plan in advance will save you a lot of headaches if anything were to occur. To create an emergency plan, check the following items:

- **Main Water Shutoff Valve**

  Know where your main water shutoff valve is located. In the event of a serious leak or flood, being able to shut off the main water valve quickly will save you from costly or even irreparable water damage.

- **Electrical Panel**

  Make sure you're also able to locate the electrical panel and label all the circuit breakers, so you know the parts of the electrical system to which they correspond.

- **Main Gas Line Shutoff Valve**

  You want to familiarize yourself with the main gas line shutoff valve. Few things are as dangerous as a gas leak in your home, and it's vitally important to be able to quickly shut off the

gas.
- **Emergency Contact List**
  Make sure to maintain an emergency contact list and to include a certified plumber, an electrician, your insurance agent, your HOA and condo association representative, and your utility providers.

Create a Plan to Pay Off Your Mortgage as Quickly as Possible

If you took out a mortgage to buy your home, as most homeowners do, it's important that you have a plan to pay off that debt as quickly as you can. Some financial advisers will tell you to prioritize any extra income you have for retirement savings (or other types of investing) before trying to pay off your mortgage early. This advice relies on the assumption that stock market returns will outpace your mortgage interest rate. This assumption may not always apply, so you should consider the other factors and how they impact your personal finances.

First, stocks are inherently risky; high returns on stocks are compensation for the risk. While your stock returns may exceed your mortgage interest in a bull market, this may not be the case in an economic downturn. Chances are, your mortgage has a fixed rate, whereas the stock market's return varies wildly and unpredictably. Paying off your mortgage in advance of the term offers guaranteed savings on interest costs. Tax laws can change, too, meaning you may not always be able to rely on the mortgage interest write-off.

Second, there is an unquantifiable value in knowing you own your home in full. Being debt free in your home provides a lot of financial independence. When the economy is in a downturn, it can be comforting to know that the cost of the roof over your head is limited to property taxes and insurance, without a monthly mortgage payment. As the famous entrepreneur Kevin O'Leary said, "If you want to find financial freedom, you need to retire all debt—and yes, that includes your mortgage."[12]

Before building a plan to pay off your mortgage early, ask yourself these two questions:

- **Do I have enough excess funds to do it?**
  Don't drain your rainy-day cash fund just so you can pay off your mortgage. However, if you have enough extra money to save, put that money toward paying off your mortgage so you can own your greatest investment in full.
- **Do I have any high-interest debt?**
  You should weigh the interest rates against each other. If you have credit card debt or student loans, those interest rates are likely higher than your mortgage. That means you'll be making more money if you pay off the high-interest debt first. In the words of Mark Cuban, renowned self-made billionaire: "Whatever in-

12   Emmie Martin, "Mark Cuban and Kevin O'Leary Agree That This Is the Best Thing to Do with Your Money," CNBC, June 27, 2018, https://www.cnbc.com/2018/06/26/why-mark-cuban-and-kevin-oleary-say-to-get-out-of-debt.html.

terest rate you have—it might be a student loan with a 7 percent interest rate; if you pay off that loan, you're making 7 percent. That's your immediate return, which is a lot safer than trying to pick a stock or trying to pick real estate, or whatever it may be."[13]

To reach financial independence, I urge you to create an emergency fund and pay off your debts, starting with the smaller ones and working your way up. As mentioned previously, I'd recommend reading David Ramsey's *The Total Money Makeover*, in which he creates seven baby steps to becoming debt free, including paying off your mortgage.

You've achieved a huge milestone by purchasing your home. However, remember to maintain your financial obligations and not to neglect the smaller details when it comes to maintenance. This way, you'll fully utilize your hard-earned investment, minimize any potential depreciation, and reap its full benefits.

---

13   Kathleen Elk, "Mark Cuban: This Is 'the Best Investment You Can Make,'" CNBC, April 16, 2018, https://www.cnbc.com/2018/04/16/mark-cuban-paying-off-credit-cards-and-debt-is-the-best-investment.html.

Chapter 8:

Home Buying Recommendations

Real estate cannot be lost or stolen, nor can it be carried away. Purchased with common sense, paid for in full, and managed with reasonable care, it is about the safest investment in the world.
— Franklin D. Roosevelt

As I mentioned in the introduction, if you don't plan on reading this entire book, or you're just looking for a few quick tips and suggestions, I would recommend reading this chapter at the very least. While most of the items mentioned here will be more useful to you with the background from the preceding chapters, the information here is the most essential. The following are the tips and tricks that I've learned throughout my career, and the least I can do is share is the knowledge.

Recommendations Before You Buy

Play the Long Game

Buying a home is a long-term commitment, so plan accordingly. Buying a home and selling it in a year or two can end up costing a lot of money once you factor in the closing costs, commissions, and other potential expenses associated with buying and selling property.

Use a Real Estate Agent

At the risk of sounding repetitive, buying a home is the most expensive purchase most people make in their life. There is a lot of paperwork to navigate, so why not let a professional help you with all the details? Typically, the seller is paying for the buyer's agent, so it doesn't cost you a thing.

Interview Your Real Estate Agent

Like any other profession, there are good and bad agents. Make sure the agent you select has adequate experience and knows what they're doing before you take any advice from them. Don't pick an agent just because they're a close family friend or relative. Find an agent who understands your needs, is experienced in the local market, and can provide you with the best advice.

Don't Become "House Poor"

Make sure you're choosing a home that fits your budget. Don't place yourself at risk of having such an expensive house that you can't afford to pay for anything else.

Calculate the Added Costs of Homeownership
Do your homework and make sure you understand all the costs of buying *other* than the sale price, such as HOA/condo dues, taxes, utilities, and insurance. Make sure you can fit these added expenses into your budget.

Check for State or Local Assistance Programs
It's worth your time to do some research. You may qualify for certain assistance programs that can make the home buying process much easier and more affordable.

Recommendations While You Buy

Know the Neighborhood
Stop by the home during the morning, midday, and at night so you get a feel for the neighborhood. Test your commute to work from the house during rush hour to make sure it is something you can deal with on a daily basis. Find out how far the nearest grocery store and other services are. Even if you don't have kids, research the quality of nearby schools as this information can affect the value of your home when you plan on selling.

Price Isn't Everything
Make sure the deal works for you holistically; don't

get stuck on just the price. For example, a higher overall price with closing cost assistance may actually be cheaper for you as a buyer. Think about the bottom line.

Negotiate
Don't underestimate the power of negotiating! You'd be surprised at what price and terms sellers may accept, depending on their needs. Consult with your agent to make informed offers.

Ask for Closing Cost Assistance
In your offer, ask for a 2 percent to 4 percent concession paid toward your closing costs. This will allow you to put more money down toward your principal, saving you thousands in interest payments over the term of your loan. Make sure to check with your lender on the maximum allowable concession amount they will accept toward closing costs.

Schedule Closing at the Beginning of the Month
If you can schedule your closing at the start of the month, you'll pay more prepaid interest at closing. Timing your closing this way will allow you to skip two monthly mortgage payments because the first payment can be paid at closing. As a result, your first payment will be due after a full month has passed, giving you anywhere from forty-five to sixty days before you need to make a mortgage payment.

Understand the Added Costs of an Older Home

Sometimes the cheapest option isn't the least expensive. If you're buying an older home, do your homework on the added costs of maintaining or repairing the home. Typically, repairs and costs that are not cosmetic such as replacing windows, a roof, or the HVAC unit do not add value to a property but rather merely preserve its value. Not preforming these repairs may hinder the value of your property though.

Consider a Townhome or Single-Family Home

Condos typically have high condo fees associated with them. Those fees provide essential services like elevator maintenance, common area maintenance and janitorial services, security, and other potential accommodations. Those fees are not like a gym membership that you can cancel at any time, though; they'll be a part of your monthly expenses. If you aren't planning on using those amenities, consider a townhome or single-family home you can grow into and not have to worry about those added costs.

Always Perform a Home Inspection

Performing a home inspection can save you tens of thousands of dollars or, better yet, deter you from buying a property with serious defects. If the home inspection turns up any issues, ask the seller to fix them or provide a credit at closing for the items listed in the property condition report.

Make a List with Deadline Dates

There are a lot of dates and time frames you need to track when purchasing a property. After signing a purchase and sale agreement, spend ten minutes making a list of the milestones or dates in chronological order, so you know what you need to do and when to do it.

Compare Mortgage Lenders

Don't settle for just any lender. Picking the right mortgage lender can make a substantial difference in interest rates and other loan terms in the long run. Make sure to work with a qualified mortgage officer.

Consider a Thirty-Year Fixed Mortgage

There are countless articles, videos, and opinions on why a fifteen-year mortgage is better than a thirty-year mortgage and vice versa. My preference is to opt for a thirty-year fixed mortgage but commit to paying it off in fifteen years. You'll end up paying off the mortgage on the home in fifteen years anyway if you're consistent with payments. However, if a life-changing event occurs, you won't be stuck with the larger monthly payments of a fifteen-year mortgage.

Understand How Your Mortgage Works

Before picking a mortgage, make sure you understand the fundamentals of different mortgage types. Consider how monthly payments are calculated, along with interest, principal, and escrow reserves. You'll be surprised how simple it is.

Plan for Expenses You'll Incur after Move-In

Save some money aside for any maintenance or improvements (painting, plumbing, etc.) that you may not have caught during the walk-throughs and inspections. You may also need to purchase furniture and add your personal finishing touches to make your house a home, so account for that as well.

Recommendations after You Buy

Keep a Fire Extinguisher in the Kitchen

It may sound like a minor detail, but you should keep a fire extinguisher in the kitchen. After all, 49 percent of home fires are caused by kitchen accidents. The cost of a fire extinguisher is minuscule compared to the possible physical and emotional trauma and property damages that could result from a fire.

Purchase a Home Warranty

Even if you completed a home inspection prior to closing, protect yourself by purchasing a home warranty for at least the first year of ownership in case any unfound defects arise. You can also try to negotiate this as a seller cost in your purchase and sale agreement.

Perform Regular Maintenance

Don't push off important maintenance items when they come up. Postponing maintenance could create larger problems down the road.

Assign a Limited Power of Attorney

Designate someone you trust to manage, rent, or sell your home in the event that you are unable to do so yourself. Safeguard your most valuable asset against the worst-case scenario.

Execute a Last Will and Testament

Ensuring you have a last will and testament, with specific instructions on what to do with your home, is crucial not only to you but your loved ones. The way your home is titled may be a major factor in how the asset is handled after your passing. Check your state laws and consult with an attorney on how to best prepare.

Pay Extra Every Month

Paying an extra $100, $200, or $300 a month beyond your minimum mortgage payment will save you thousands in interest and shorten the term to pay off your loan by years. Just make sure your loan terms don't have any penalties for early payments.

Pay Off Your Mortgage Early

If you have the money to pay off your mortgage early, you'll end up freeing cash flow every month. Some argue that you shouldn't pay off your mortgage early because you can deduct the interest from your taxes, but as historical tax reforms have shown, that may not always be a reliable incentive. Additionally, you may lose more money to interest than you'd be able to write off on taxes. As the famous entrepreneur Kevin O'Leary says, "If you want to find financial freedom, you need to retire all debt—and yes, that includes your mortgage."

Appendix A
Home Buying Timeframe

The best time to buy a home is always five years ago.
—Ray Brown

Buying a home is a long-term commitment, and for that reason, most buyers will want to take their time to make sure they are making an informed decision. According to Zillow, it takes an average of four and a half months to sign a purchase and sale agreement on a home.[14] Additionally, you can expect it to take one to two months to close on a home once under contract. Like anything else in the home buying process, the timeline can vary dramatically, depending on your specific situation and market conditions. The following is a breakdown of about how long each step in the home buying process should take.

---

14   "First-Time Buyers, Here Is Your Buying a House Timeline," Trulia Guides, Trulia, accessed September 24, 2019, https://www.trulia.com/guides/buying-a-house-timeline/.

Preparing Your Finances: Six to Nine Months

If you're financially stable and have enough saved for a down payment, you may not need to prepare your finances. However, most buyers will need to plan for this milestone. During the financial planning phase, you should:

- save as much as possible for your down payment;
- understand your financial situation by creating a budget and calculating your debt-to-income ratio;
- understand the costs associated with home-ownership;
- work on improving your credit score;
- understand the various types of mortgages; and
- talk to a certified financial adviser and loan officer.

Finding Your Home and Making an Offer: Three to Five Months

According to a Zillow research report, about 50 percent of home buyers searched for a home for less than three months, 37 percent searched for less than six months, and 13 percent shopped for seven months to a year.[15] During the period in which you're searching for a home and making an offer, you should:

- interview real estate agents and sign an agency

15 "The Zillow Group Report on Consumer Housing Trends," Zillow Research, Zillow, accessed November 22, 2017, https://www.zillow.com/research/zillow-group-report-2016-13279/.

agreement;
- search for properties online that fit your budget;
- visit and tour properties in person;
- understand market fundamentals, value, and home stats; and
- make an offer on a house that you feel comfortable calling home.

Post Ratified Contract: Thirty to Forty-Five Days

There are a lot of important items that need to be completed during the short time frame post ratified contract. The road to closing may be long and daunting. During your study period, you should:
- continuously communicate with your lender and provide the necessary documentation to get approved for your loan;
- send a check to your escrow agent with your earnest money deposit;
- schedule a home inspection and appraisal;
- review the home inspection report and negotiate repairs or credits needed with the seller;
- shop for homeowner's insurance; and
- waive any other contingencies in your purchase and sale agreement.

Closing: Seven to Ten Days

Closing is a one-day event, but preparing for closing can take anywhere from seven to ten days. To make it to closing, you'll want to:
- perform a final inspection of the property;
- inform the title company of how you want to

take title to your property;
- review the settlement statement and closing documents;
- wire the remaining balance owed; and
- get the keys to your new home.

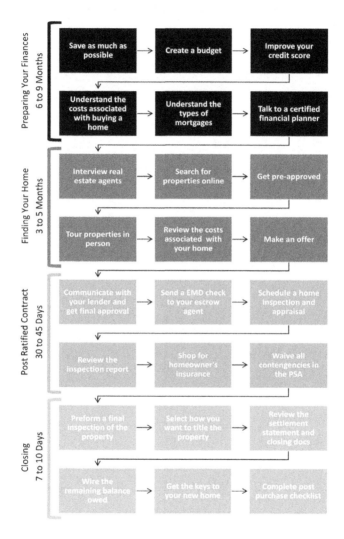

Figure 8: *Home Buying Timeframe*

Appendix B
Acronyms List

ARM: Adjustable-Rate Mortgage
CD: Closing Disclosure
CMA: Comparative Market Analysis
DOM: Days on Market
EMD: Earnest Money Deposit
FHA Loan: Federal Housing Administration
HOA: Homeowner's Association
HVAC: Heating, Ventilation, and Air Conditioning
PCR: Property Condition Report
PMI: Primary Mortgage Insurance
PSA: Purchase and Sale Agreement
USDA Loan: a loan provided by the United States Department of Agriculture
USPS: United States Postal Service
VA Loan: a loan provided by the United States Department of Veterans Affairs

Appendix C
Glossary

appraisal: An estimate of the value of your home provided by a certified appraiser.

capital gains: Profit made from the sale of a property.

closing costs: The expenses, above the price of the property, that buyers and sellers normally incur to complete a real estate transaction.

closing disclosure: A form that provides final details on the closing costs and mortgage for your home. It includes loan terms, your projected monthly payments, and how much you will pay in fees and other costs to close on the property.

comparative market analysis: An estimate of a home's value based on recently sold, similar properties in the immediate area.

contingency: A contingency clause defines a condition or action that must be met for a real estate contract to become binding.

debt-to-income ratio: A personal financial measurement that looks at the total debt you have compared to your overall income.

earnest money deposit: A deposit made to a seller that represents a buyer's good faith to buy a home.

escrow: An account where money is held by a third party on behalf of two other parties until the transaction is completed.

home inspection: A noninvasive examination of the condition of a home, often in connection with the sale of that home.

home warranty: A service contract that covers the cost of maintaining household systems or appliances for a set period of time (typically one year).

homeowner's association (HOA): An organization in a subdivision, planned community, or condominium building that makes and enforces rules for the properties and residents. Those who purchase property within an HOA's jurisdiction automatically become members and are required to pay dues, known as HOA fees.

homeowner's insurance: A form of property insurance that covers losses and damages to an individual's residence, including furnishings and other assets in the home.

interest: Money paid regularly at a particular rate for the use of borrowed from a lender.

last will and testament: A legal document that communicates a person's final wishes pertaining to assets and dependents.

mortgage: A debt instrument, secured by the collateral of specified real estate property, that the borrower is obliged to pay back with a predetermined set of payments.

opportunity cost: The loss of potential gain from other alternatives when one alternative is chosen.

power of attorney: A legal document giving authoritative power to someone to act on behalf of another person in specified legal or financial matters.

principal: The original sum of money borrowed in a loan.

property condition report: An evaluation of the current safety condition and capital expenses that will likely be required to maintain an asset in the short- and long-term.

purchase and sale agreement: A binding legal contract that obligates a buyer to buy and a seller to sell a property.

settlement date: The date when a trade is final and the buyer must make payment to the seller while the seller delivers the property title.

settlement statement: A document that summarizes the terms and conditions of a settlement. It provides full disclosure of a loan's terms and details of all the fees and charges that a borrower must pay.

title: The legal ownership and legal right to use and enjoy a piece of property.

title insurance: Title insurance protects real estate owners and lenders against any property loss or damage they might experience because of liens, encumbrances, or defects in the title to the property.

Acknowledgments

When I started writing this book, I did not realize the amount of people it would take to make it a reality. Each of the people below helped me instrumentality in one way or another to the success of this book.

Sara Assaf: My wife, editor, and biggest support system. I could not have done it without you. I love you!

Irfan and Ghazwa Totonji: My parents, who taught me everything I know and then some. You are the best human beings alive!

Abdulrahman and Iman Totonji: My siblings, and the people I confide in most. Thank you for everything!

William Gray: A teacher in every way. I've learned so much from you over the years about real estate investments and more importantly life.

Brian Grindall: One of the greatest professors I've ever had, who continues to teach me to this day.

Fouad Talout: My first mentor who guided me through my first sale and continues to inspire me every day.

Dick Bryan: A scholar, a gentleman, and the most humble man alive. You believed in me from the beginning.

Young You: My most trusted colleague. I cherish your advice more then you know!

Muhammad Kandil: A friend I can count on, who I will one day beat in tennis.

Ali Alaswadi: A wise and dependable friend, who teaches me something new every time we talk.

About the Author

Abduljabar Totonji, also known as "Jabs," is a real estate investor, developer, property manager, and licensed real estate agent. He graduated from George Mason University with a bachelor's degree in economics and completed his master's degree in real estate finance at Georgetown University. Jabs has acquired, sold, managed, and advised on over one billion dollars in commercial and residential real estate transactions.

Bibliography

"Nation's Population Growth Slowed This Decade," The United States Census Bureau, accessed on April 6, 2020, www.census.gov/library/stories/2020/04/nations-population-growth-slowed-this-decade.html.

"Historical Census of Housing Tables," The United States Census Bureau, accessed on August 25, 2019, www.census.gov/housing/census/data/values.html.

"What Is a Good Credit Score," Ask Experian, Experian, accessed April 16, 2020, www.experian.com/blogs/ask-experian/credit-education/score-basics/what-is-a-good-credit-score/.

Clarke, Katherine. "Billionaire Ken Griffin Buys America's Most Expensive Home for $238 Million." The Wall Street Journal, Dow Jones & Company, January 23, 2019, www.wsj.com/articles/billionaire-ken-griffin-buys-americas-most-expensive-home-for-238-million-11548271301.

Bach, David. *The Automatic Millionaire: a Powerful One-Step Plan to Live and Finish Rich* (New

York: Currency Press, 2016)

Stanley, Thomas J. and William D. Danko, *The Millionaire Next Door: The Surprising Secrets of America's Wealthy* (Lanham, MD: Taylor Trade Publishing, 1996)

"Selling Guide." B3-6-02, Debt-to-Income Ratios, Fannie Mae, accessed February 5, 2020, selling-guide.fanniemae.com/Selling-Guide/Origination-thru-Closing/Subpart-B3-Underwriting-Borrowers/Chapter-B3-6-Liability-Assessment/1032992131/B3-6-02-Debt-to-Income-Ratios-02-05-2020.htm.

"About Fannie Mae & Freddie Mac," Federal Housing Finance Agency, accessed May 20,2020, www.fhfa.gov/SupervisionRegulation/FannieMae-andFreddieMac/Pages/About-Fannie-Mae---Freddie-Mac.aspx.

Ramsey, Dave, *The Total Money Makeover: a Proven Plan for Financial Fitness* (Nashville, TN: Thomas Nelson, Inc., 2013),

Mohammed, Riyadh, "Hot Trend in 2017: Rise of Islamic Banks on Main St. USA." *CNBC*, December 5, 2016, www.cnbc.com/2016/12/02/under-the-radar-islamic-banks-rise-in-th.html.

"How to Make an Offer on a House," Home Buyers Guide, Zillow, accessed December 20, 2019, www.zillow.com/home-buying-guide/making-an-offer-on-a-house/.

"How Long Does It Take to Buy a House? 6 Fast Steps," Home Buyers Guide, Zillow, accessed on February 8, 2020, www.zillow.com/home-buying-guide/how-long-does-it-take-to-buy-a-house/.

"Cooking," Public Education, National Fire Protection Association, accessed on July 1, 2020 www.nfpa.org/Public-Education/Fire-causes-and-risks/Top-fire-causes/Cooking.

"Mail Forwarding Options," FAQs, United States Postal Services, August 1, 2020, faq.usps.com/s/article/Mail-Forwarding-Options.

Martin, Emmie, "Mark Cuban and Kevin O'Leary Agree That This Is the Best Thing to Do with Your Money," *CNBC*, June 27, 2018, www.cnbc.com/2018/06/26/why-mark-cuban-and-kevin-oleary-say-to-get-out-of-debt.html.

Elk, Kathleen, "Mark Cuban: This Is 'the Best Investment You Can Make,'" *CNBC*, April 16, 2018, www.cnbc.com/2018/04/16/mark-cuban-paying-off-credit-cards-and-debt-is-the-best-investment.html.

"First-Time Buyers, Here Is Your Buying a House Timeline," Trulia Guides, Trulia, accessed on September 24, 2019, www.trulia.com/guides/buying-a-house-timeline/.

"The Zillow Group Report on Consumer Housing Trends," Zillow Research, Zillow, accessed on November 22, 2018 www.zillow.com/research/zillow-group-report-2016-13279/.

Made in United States
North Haven, CT
30 August 2023

40937958R00078